10/29/14

SELF-LOVE

A Gift you Give Yourself

DR. KATHERINE E. JAMES

authorHOUSE®

AuthorHouse™
1663 Liberty Drive
Bloomington, IN 47403
www.authorhouse.com
Phone: 1 (800) 839-8640

Published by AuthorHouse 09/22/2016

ISBN: 978-1-5246-4080-4 (sc)
ISBN: 978-1-5246-4079-8 (hc)
ISBN: 978-1-5246-4078-1 (e)

Library of Congress Control Number: 2016915626

Print information available on the last page.

DEDICATION

This book is dedicated to my mother, Yvonne Woods. I am who I am because of who you were. Thank you for being a wonderful mother. I always like to say, you were not perfect, but you were perfect for me. You loved me well! Because of that I know how to love well.

I miss you momma …

Dedication, also, to my wonderful husband Kim who never hinders me from flowing in my areas of giftedness. Thank you for loving me as you do, without demand that I be other than I am. I love you, honey!

Finally, to my son, Kim Jr. You are my precious gift from God. My love for you is more than I could ever demonstrate; it is overwhelmingly larger than life. And to my heart, daughter Amanda. I appreciate the love you have for Kim Jr., and I love how you have become my precious daughter.

FOREWORD

My dear friend and colleague, Dr. Kathy James, has done two wonderfully instructive and supportive things for me in *Self-Love*: She has made me a better teacher and coach of writing, and she has made me better appreciate the concept of self-love just for myself.

One of the challenges I regularly face is getting students and clients to shed negative self-imagery of their writing abilities. Often these individuals have been told and shown in painfully relentless regularity that their writing abilities are hopelessly subpar and, absent a miracle, unlikely to improve.

Through the experiences (and honor) of assisting Dr. James with the editing of *Self-Love*, I stumbled upon several gems of wisdom and insight that I've found directly helpful. Particularly powerful is her gentle yet thorough guiding of the reader to "tell the whole truth" about yourself, to yourself. For a developing writer, following such sage advice can help separate truth from fiction about one's abilities. While I have previously applied a version of this in my consultations with students and clients, Dr. Kathy provides in *Self-Love* a helpful and structured way to go about doing this even more meaningfully.

...and something else...

Her willingness to be vulnerable, to be transparent throughout the narrative both exemplifies courage *and* inspires courage to face down the demons of self-doubts and self-delusion. One cannot sincerely engage this reading without coming away transformed. It is this transformational mindedness that I intend to pour into my students and clients; individuals who need desperately to find the excellent writer fighting for life in their scarred intellectual souls.

Thank you for this book, my dear friend. May God's greatest blessings bring all that you deserve, need, and want!

Dr. Robert McTyre, Sr., September 10, 2016

FOREWORD

I first met Dr. Katherine James in the spring of 1989. At that time I only knew her as Mrs. Katherine James, a caring lady who was acting as a support person to her nephew who had been placed by social service into my care. She exhibited genuine love and concern for her nephew and allowed him to spend time with her on the weekends. In December of that same year I began pastoring and "Kathy" was my first member, thus we began a twenty seven year relationship as ministry partners and friends. So it is with great delight and a sense of tremendous honor that I write the foreword to her new book "Self-Love". This book is a natural for Kathy because she does not have to make anything up. She writes from personal experience as she has taken and continues to take her journey into "Self-Love", the type of love that God desires all of us to walk in.

Until we have come to love ourselves, we will never be able to love others as God would have us to. Kathy's educational experiences (Associates Degree, Bachelor's Degree, two Masters Degrees and a PhD) added to her personal quest for self-love makes her extremely qualified to walk us through the journey of discovering and living with an accurate understanding of "self-love".

This book will help you to find the path to self-love, and if you are already on the path it will help you along the way. One of the greatest challenges people face today is really knowing, how to love themselves. This is clearly seen in the lifestyle choices so many make, where individuals often abuse themselves and others.

In this book Dr. James defines self-love in a very simple, yet profound way. You will be able to easily grasp the concepts and principles of self-love and yet not fill as though they are reading a graduate level psychology text. Dr. James walks us through the process of self-love while sharing her personal journey and the discoveries she has made along the way.

I have always thought of myself as one who loved himself, yet while reading "Self-Love" I gained new understanding and insight into the fact that knowing one's self and loving one's self, is truly one of the keys to living a fulfilled life. Knowing God and loving Him is a given.

Each chapter gives progressive action steps designed to take us from where we are in our self-love journey to where we desire to be. Dr. James guides us into how to know ourselves better, loving ourselves where we are and moving forward from there, knowing our strengths and weaknesses and the impact they have on us. Dr. James also discusses the critical role self-forgiveness plays in the whole process.

After reading "Self -Love", I am now more ready to appreciate and celebrate the unique person that God has created me to be. As you read, I am positive this book will have a similar impact on your life, as you learn to love and live better.

Apostle Bobby Bracy
Senior Pastor
Shiloh Deliverance Church

CONTENTS

CHAPTER ONE

SELF-LOVE

Imagine a high school with hundreds of teens going in and out of classrooms, cafeterias, walking the hallways and entering forbidden staff-only passages. Some are experiencing their first year, while others are nearing the end of their high school journeys. What are the challenges faced by this multitude? There are many ...

Now fast forward some thirty years later. Those teens of the past are now nearing the fifty-year mark. Where (how) do we find them? Perhaps they are still in high school hallways, classrooms, or staff designated areas. Only now they move about in adult forms – parents, grandparents, community leaders, and faculty or staff members. What are the challenges faced by this multitude? Again, there are many ...

Life expectations suggest a stark difference between the challenges faced by the high school students, compared to those experienced by the almost fifty year olds. In many cases this would be an accurate assessment. Consider some of the challenges: The teen wrestles with initial romantic encounters, while the fifty year old struggles with romance maintenance (keeping it alive amidst life's demands) or recovery after the end of it – divorce; the teen's thoughts of the future center on whether to attend college or not, while the fifty year old ponders mid-life career changes. How to make a difference in the lives of others (leaving a legacy) is a likely thought of the elder, while much of the teen's mental energy focuses on what she wants and what makes her happy.

In a sense, the struggles are similar, yet when viewed through the lens of life's stages, they are starkly different – at least the potential consequences are. There is one challenge however, that looms large in both life periods. Consider this...the teen who never really learned to love herself very likely – at fifty – has not learned to love who she is today.

The absence of self-love is one of life's greatest tragedies!

An increase in your capacity to love yourself is my hope as you journey through this dialogue on self-love.

LOVE

When speaking of love, I am not referencing this madness that leads to willful abandonment of one's good senses. Love is not an animalistic lust that leads to the pursuit of sexual desires at any cost. It is not a euphoric experience that can be easily turned on today and off tomorrow, fueled by the emotions of experiences and expectations. Nor is it the need to be with, possess, or conquer the person of our dreams or (all too often) nightmares. These ways of being are NOT love. They are but a semblance of one of the most powerfully rewarding states a high school teen, fifty year old, or any human could ever achieve.

Love is the greatest gift we can give ourselves and ultimately others. Hopefully, by now you are asking the obvious : What is love?

A review of literature leaves us with many definitions for this very powerful word. For the purposes of our journey, however, I offer the following explanation of love:

> Love is an authentic acceptance and valuing of a person
> in the moment without demand of otherness. *Basically it*
> *means you are accepted and valued just as you are.*

When we truly love, we authentically (genuinely) accept and value. Consider engaging a newborn baby. We certainly don't demand or expect of them and yet we freely give the best we have to offer - We love! Loving an infant without demand is absolutely necessary if they are to grow into an emotionally healthy individual, this is rather obvious. Perhaps not so apparent is the need for this kind of love throughout life. We are emotionally healthier when we love ourselves in this manner and when we experience this kind of love from others. Authentic acceptance and valuing is also a precursor to healthy change. It is the unspoken motivation to become our better selves.

Through this lens of self-love, we come to understand and appreciate that love (authentic acceptance and valuing) is not a license to remain stagnate, to shirk responsibility to self and others, or to continue to do that which is not beneficial – like mistreating others with the excuse "this is just the way that I am." This statement may seem contradictory to the notion of "without demand of otherness." There is treasure inherent in the act of accepting and valuing humans just because we are. This attitude is fertile ground for being ok with whom we are today, while also moving toward becoming our better selves.

Throughout the book, you will notice that I employ inclusive language (we and us). Not only am I writing to help others learn to better love themselves, but I too must continue growing in this area. Thus, while speaking to you, I am also reminding myself of the need to continually increase this gift in my life. Now on to self-love …

SELF-LOVE

Self-love is an accepting, valuing and embracing of one's entire self, inclusive of an activating awareness, which motivates toward the need to continually change for the better.

This notion of self-love is so important to healthy living that my definition of it bears repeating. Self-love is an accepting, valuing and embracing of one's entire self, inclusive of an activating awareness, which motivates towards the need to continually change for the better.

In other words, while I recognize the need to keep getting better, I love and celebrate who I am now.

NOTE: Self-loathing conversation is never acceptable. Honesty is always acceptable, but how we say something is sometimes more important than what we say. For example: in speaking to me, it is acceptable to say "Kathy that wasn't a nice thing you did." It is never acceptable to say, "Kathy you are a horrible [or use any self-defeating term] person for the thing you did." I certainly believe we must be honest with ourselves if we are going to improve, but negative self-talk does not help the process; it hinders the process of change. While engaging in this type of behavior, you become your own road block. Is this your intention? Probably not.

Increasing levels of self-love compels us to better our best. Why? Because at the core, humans are created with an inherent nature to grow and become; perhaps more importantly humans are created with purpose. There is a connection between loving ourselves and pursuing purpose. When we love ourselves, we are continually checking to see if we are living on purpose rather than haphazardly existing. As self-love grows, we are increasingly uncomfortable with being out of alignment with our life's purpose. There is a continual inner compelling to better our best – to be intentional about the process of becoming who we are destined to be. Achieving purpose is a lifelong pursuit. Having life means that we have the opportunity to become our better selves.

A SHORT WORD ON PURPOSE ...

The market is filled with books written on the subject of purpose – Rick Warren's *A Purpose Drive Life*" and Myles Monroe's *In Pursuit of Purpose*, both are good reads on this subject. To that end, I don't feel a need to have an extensive conversation on the subject. However, I believe a brief mentioning is warranted.

This notion of purpose can seem elusive or out of reach. Many struggle with answering the question, "What is my purpose?" My response to this question is simply this: your purpose in life is the very reason you exist. Chances are, in some ways, you are tapping into elements of purpose. Consider or ask yourself the following: (1) What do I most enjoy doing? (2) What would I do for free? (3) I feel most fulfilled when ... (4) How would I spend my last week on earth? Your responses to these types of questions provide insight into purpose.

Humans are not created to do one thing. Our life's purpose is better viewed as a common theme, easily identified throughout our life's course. What is your common theme?

For example, my common theme is helping others become their "*better selves.*"

As a family member and friend, I try really hard to...

- Love others well, by being with them (physical and psychological presence), by listening to them and holding their confidences when beneficial, by talking to them in life-affirming ways, by speaking the truth in love (for their benefit, not mine), by celebrating their triumphs and mourning their defeats, and by sharing my time, possessions, skills and talents, thoughts and ideas, hopes and dreams, struggles and defeats. In essence, I give of myself to them ... aiding in the process of them becoming their "better selves."

As a professional (pastor, therapist, professor, public speaker, student advisor, distance learning technologist, mentor and author), it is my goal to give my very best at all times ...

- I personally believe it is a privilege to serve others, that relationships are tremendous gifts when built on mutual respect and honor. I don't allow my credentials to delude me into believing that I have some inherent right to speak into the lives of others because I have earned an Associates, Bachelors, two Masters and a PhD. These accomplishments have undoubtedly opened doors and paved the way for me to function in most of these roles. But to believe that I have some right because of them is arrogant and belittling of the preciousness of every human regardless of past or present acts, socio- economic status, ethnic affiliation, gender or age.

I work to be my best most of the time, understanding that my best changes on a daily basis. On a scale of negative one to a positive ten, today I may be a positive 10, tomorrow I may be a negative one (-1). The gift I offer is learning to be okay in both states. I am not always functioning at a 10 nor am I constantly functioning at a -1, and both states are acceptable. When we learn to be okay in our current states, we can get about the business of *bettering our best* rather than engaging in justification, denial, avoidance and self-deceptive behaviors.

Again I take this short detour to talk about purpose because it is directly connected to this notion of self-love. Increased self-love manifests purposeful living! Now, ask yourself this question - be completely honest, there is no right or wrong answer, only a question with the goal of self-awareness:

How do you feel about yourself? Or, what do you think about yourself? Does it resemble self-love as described above?

If it does, I celebrate you and encourage you to share your story of achieving your current level of self-love. This sharing is NOT for the goal of self-glorification or any narcissistic purpose. In fact, if either is consciously or subconsciously your goal, I suspect your level of self-love is limited, and probably lower than you have allowed yourself to believe. When we operate from a healthy level of self-love we are less likely to function in narcissistic ways. From a perspective of self-love, the goal of sharing with others is primarily for their benefit, in order for them to get a glimpse of self-love and thereby embark on their own personal journey to gain or increase one of life's greatest treasures – SELF LOVE which is…

an accepting, valuing and embracing of one's entire self,
inclusive of an activating awareness which motivates toward
the need to continually change for the better.

We owe it to ourselves, loved ones and those we have the privilege of encountering to pursue this precious gift of self-love.

Words of Consideration or Caution

The pursuit of self-love offers opportunities of life-changing experiences. Since the result of self-love is tangibly noticeable, this journey takes varying levels of courage. To that end, it's important to be aware of several things:

❖ Those closest to us may be the last to notice our changes. Think about it this way. You see your son daily and haven't noticed that he is four inches taller. However, his aunt, who hasn't seen him in six weeks, immediately recognizes the difference. There are times when those closest to us legitimately or conveniently do not recognize our changes.

❖ You are a part of a system. When you change, the system will be impacted and will inevitably change. The system parts (family members, friends, co-workers etc.) may prefer the status quo – the old you. In this instance there is likely to be some resistance to your pursuit of self-love. This is normal, not necessarily beneficial, but to be expected. Humans are generally averse to change and prefer the current state, even if it isn't the best situation. Be patient with them; you willingly walked into this process of transformation. They, on the other hand, were drafted by your choice to change.

❖ Some people may hinder your journey by their inability to add value to the process. "There are those who are simply not good for us on this journey and we may have to love them from a distance" (Bracy, 2013).

❖ Courage is also required because pursuing increased levels of self-love requires us to step out of our comfort zones into *unknown places of you*. We must soberly look at all that we are, think, and do and be honest about the discovery.

❖ Finally, it is important for us to believe that there is a unique purpose for our existence. With that in mind, we might as well get about the business of uncovering our unique reasons for being.

STARTING WHERE YOU ARE

The practice of loving one's self can begin at any time in life. It is never too early or too late to start loving yourself better. Self-love is such a priceless gift that one cannot allow history to decide if it is to be achieved. The present situation is not worth robbing from a daily diet of self-valuing and acceptance. More than that, any possible future is guaranteed to be better as one learns to give the gift of self-love.

ABOUT ME … WHAT FOSTERED VALUE AND THE PURSUIT OF SELF-LOVE?

My childhood memories are filled with being with family, and going to grandma's house. My mom was the oldest of seven girls, with two older brothers. Shortly after my birth one of my mom's brothers died. About five years later, the oldest of the clan, uncle Leroy, was killed. As a result, my childhood memories are filled with experiences of strong Black women taking care of life's business.

We grew up in Detroit. In today's terms our standard of living would be described as impoverished. However, my recollection of childhood brings to mind many things, but experiences of poverty are not amongst them. In fact, although money was scarce, there was little about my childhood experience that was impoverished. It's amazing how children are shielded from many of life's onslaughts when those in charge love them and are responsible. My family's matriarchs were loving and fairly responsible. Their acts transmitted wonderful life-giving messages of worth to us children. One of those earliest unspoken messages was that children are special and the adults in their lives are privileged, not burdened, by the care of them. This is not to portray perfection; by this I mean, my family's matriarchs were and are far from being perfect. However, I somehow sensed that their acts (good, bad and ugly; mistakes and accomplishments) were intended for our good.

So here is how I remember our childhood: other family members perhaps saw or experienced our childhood differently, but this is my reality. It is *this* truth--my truth--that shaped me. Ongoing messages of care, concern, adult responsibility and love from grandma were experienced by her determination that children had enough to eat and her open door policy, which was we were always welcomed at grandma's house. Momma consistently did her best to make sure we were taken care of. She wasn't a perfect mother, as no mom is. But I like to say she was perfect for me. I love myself and much of that credit goes to her. Mom modeled acceptance. She consistently accepted all of us as we were. This created a wonderful space for self-acceptance. Mom's acceptance fostered a desire to give my best at all times, while simultaneously allowing me to be okay with my limitations. Her influence in this area was further shaped by other matriachs in the family; my aunties.

My wonderful aunts came in varying shapes, sizes and personalities and each left an indelible mark on my childhood.

Let's start with Auntie Jackie. Prior to having children, she treated me as her own and loved on me with such diligence and power. You may think "loved on" is an odd or incorrect way of making this statement. It is intentionally stated in this way, as the phrase accurately captures how I felt.

Later in life, Aunt Pollette modeled before me what it was like to give of one's gifts and talents, as she perpetually taught me from her repertoire of life experiences (like turning a cartwheel and hitting a tennis ball). Once she learned, she (consciously or unconsciously – I don't know which) taught it to others. Neither of us knew how one unassuming afternoon of learning to turn cartwheels, would positively impact my life many years later as that skill (knowing how to turn cartwheels) helped position me to serve as captain of my high school cheer team from 10th through 12th grade. What an ego booster! More importantly, my natural leadership skills were resultantly being nurtured and solidified. Even after Aunt Pollette experienced some challenges that led to major changes, she continued to birth in me a love for school and school-related activities. She did it, so I did it! Why? Because I knew she loved me. This is not to say that my other aunts failed to do anything special for me – they all did in very unique ways. The stories of their positive impact on my life are sufficient to fill another book, "The Blessings of Aunties" – perhaps in the future.

For now, here is a snippet of my other aunties and the special qualities they embodied...

Aunt Marcella was the youngest of the group and probably the wildest. As children, both traits worked for us. We loved being around her and her children (our cousins). I fondly recall frequent visits to her ever-changing dwelling places where she welcomed my baby sister and I with open arms.

Aunt Priscilla modeled the determination to hone one's craft, use your God-given talent to make a living and follow your dreams.

Auntie Minnie was always the life of the party. She was famous for out dancing all – old and young alike. She modeled a love for life and enjoyment.

Auntie Arbutus modeled some very important aspects of the woman's role. Cooking and baking were frequent activities in her home; along with fun, music and much laughter. Oh, let me not forget to mention discipline. She was indeed a disciplinarian. From her I learned to obey the first time.

Aunt Shirley, the one sister who lived out of town, modeled the necessity of staying connected to family, no matter the distance. She, too, like Auntie Arbutus, modeled aspects of the role of a woman – cooking and hospitality.

These were all special women who gave me special attention during my formative years and, thus, directly influenced my ability to love me. In fact, if I were to write about the positive impact that so many individuals have had in my childhood--sisters, cousins, friends, neighbors and teachers--it would take volumes to complete the stories. Many people deposited gifts throughout my childhood that enabled me to possess a healthy sense of self which developed into love for self and others.

My personal experience is not the only path to self-love. I simply share it to provide a glimpse of my life's journey. However, if you didn't grow up in a family situation that fostered a sense of self love, please believe me: it is NEVER too late to achieve it. Today, in this very moment, you can begin the process of learning to love yourself better. No matter what has previously occurred in your life--what you have done, or what others have done to you--it is possible to love yourself better.

Many times I wondered about the benefit of writing this book. I wrestled with the idea there were already too many self-help books on the market, or the fact that I was not an expert on this subject of love, and that many are far more qualified to speak on this subject than I. However, when I thought about the emotional and psychological freedom I receive from accepting and valuing my good, bad and ugly--and contrasting my reality with so many individuals who are imprisoned by self-devaluing practices--the benefits became clear and my passion to write was renewed.

To that end, if only one person learns to give himself or herself the gift of love, I can confidently declare this writing journey to be well worth the cost. So let's get to it.

What determines whether or not an individual achieves a healthy sense of self-love or spends a lifetime failing to arrive at places of internal liberty, peace, and jubilee?

Perhaps the better question is... *who* determines whether or not self-love is achieved? The obvious (or perhaps not so obvious) answer is the individual. It is you and I who make the decision of whether or not we will truly love ourselves. There is an erroneous belief that others can stop us from achieving in life. Whereas there may be some level of fact in some of life's areas, when it comes to achieving self-love, unless we give this authority away, others are powerless to make this determination on our behalf. The power of choice to achieve self-love lies within each of us. In the event that we have given the authority to another, perhaps now is the time to take it back. Well let me state it in a more declarative manner. Since you are reading this book, NOW is the time to take back your power, regain your authority and secure or increase self-love in your life.

LEARNING TO ACHIEVE OR INCREASE SELF-LOVE

This book *Self-Love* is written with the intent of showing one way (not the only way) of learning to better love ourselves. The increase of self-love is not a destination at which we arrive, signaling the end of a process. It is a journey embarked upon throughout a lifetime. The diagram below provides a graphic representation of the ongoing process. We begin with self-exploration, proceeding through self-discovery, self-acceptance, self-forgiveness, self-appreciation and celebration, ultimately arriving at a deeper level of self-love. The cyclical nature of this process represents continuity and the spiraling element is representative of the achievements of deeper and deeper levels of self love (Balswick & Balswick, 1999). Each level helps to move us closer to living a life that is filled with accepting and valuing self and others. It is important to mention here that loving others is a natural outgrowth of self-love (*more about this in the final chapter*).

SELF-LOVE FORMULA

Remember this process is not linear (occurring in a this-must-happen-before-that format), but cyclical as it is designed to take us to deeper and deeper levels of self-love with each completed cycle.

Interior book images designed by Joy P. Creel

OPPORTUNITY FOR REFLECTIONS

After each section, you are given an opportunity to reflect. Ultimately, increased self-love is the goal of the book. This process takes work and time. My hope is that you would not only read the book, but engage it in such a way that you wrestle, reflect, question, dispute, and choose to accept or agree. In short, the journey asks you to do something with the previously read information. To that end, I have provided a section entitled "Opportunity for Reflections" at the end of each chapter. Here is your first opportunity to reflect about the introduction of the book. This is a suggestion. If you have nothing to reflect, feel free to ignore this section and read on. But maybe come back when something does come to you.

CHAPTER TWO

SELF-EXPLORATION

Only by much searching and mining are gold and diamonds obtained, and man can find every truth connected with his being if he will dig deep into the mine of his soul.

- James Allen

Get to know yourself better. There are many ways to approach self-exploration. Let me suggest four paths that continue to work for me: (1) Tell yourself *the whole truth,* (2) Be intentional about identifying your ever changing emotions, (3) Pay attention to your physical responses to internal and external experiences and (4) Engage in activities that will increase your relational awareness.

Please note: there is a connection between honesty and growth in this endeavor. To the degree that you are honest with yourself, the likelihood of self-love increases. So, do yourself a favor, tell yourself the whole truth. Being honest with ourselves is often not easy, but it is absolutely necessary to increase in self-love. So we will begin with a discussion about telling the truth.

TELL YOURSELF THE WHOLE TRUTH

Being honest with your self is good exercise.
- Sigmund Freud

Perhaps some of you don't resonate with this notion of lying to yourself. Well let's look at a few examples. Have you ever found yourself in a conversation with others who believed something about you that wasn't totally accurate? Perhaps, they believed you to be nicer, smarter, happier, braver, or even sadder than you actually were and for some reason you went along with it. And perhaps as this type of engagement continued you came to embrace this misjudgment and went even further by rehearsing it to yourself. If you were practicing for the benefit of change, this could be good, but if it's pretense, then not so good. If you are simply lying to yourself – stating that you are not afraid of something when in all actuality you are terrified of the possibility of its occurrence, or pretending to be free hearted and giving when in fact you greatly dislike sharing - here is an opportunity to stop deceiving yourself and others! Stop lying, speak the reality, and then declare the preferred.

For example...

A group of ladies are in support of a friend who is in the process of a divorce. The conversation suggests that she is better off and many "pats on the back" are given for her perceived strength and ease in moving through the difficult course of events (this is how the potential divorcee has presented herself). For various reasons the soon-to-be divorcee does not correct her friends by sharing her true feelings of impending doom, bouts of crying fits and absolute fear of what is to come. Instead, she carries on the act and even worse, begins to tell herself the lies. All the while, there is an internal war raging, because deep down inside she knows none of this is true. She is not brave or happy and doesn't see herself as better off. The future divorcee does not want her marriage to end; in fact, she still deeply loves her husband and is terrified of being without him.

So what is she to do? There are many choices here. However, as it relates to this notion of increased self-love, she must STOP lying to herself, SPEAK her reality and then DECLARE the preferred. This soon-to-be divorcee must stop agreeing with her friends, at the very least, speak (to herself if not her friends as well) the truth about her feelings and current state of being (e.g., I am afraid, I am sad and lonely, this hurts), and then she must declare the preferred (e.g., I don't want to be afraid; I am sad and lonely now, I want this situation to work out, I won't always be afraid, somehow things will get better).

Review

When we fail to tell ourselves and others the truth we SSD:

(1) **S**top lying
(2) **S**peak our reality-the current situation
(3) **D**eclare the preferred (how we would like life to be)

Need help?

Are you challenged with telling yourself the whole truth, with being completely honest about many of life's situations? I believe we do the best we can, given our prior experiences. I also believe that those prior experiences often lock us into unhealthy behavioral patterns, because it's all we know. It is not until we know better that we do generally do better. So, perhaps you sincerely desire to tell yourself the truth and have even attempted to follow the steps as outlined above but find that you inevitably fall back into old practices of altering the truth in order to temporarily feel better. If this describes your behavior, chances are you could benefit from professional help. A mental health practitioner who is willing to meet you where you are and walk with you towards increased wholeness could greatly benefit you on this self-love journey.

Note of Importance:

There is a stigma in our society about going to a therapist. It goes something like this, "Did you hear Kathy's seeing a counselor, what's wrong with her?" "I thought she was pastor, why doesn't she just pray about it? Isn't her God powerful enough to help with whatever she's seeing a therapist about?" "I thought she *was* a therapist. How could a therapist need a therapist?" "She must be crazy, because only crazy people go to therapy."

This kind of conversation is misguided, inaccurate and harmful. It is unlikely that a person with a knife stuck in her chest would be instructed to stay home, remove the knife and heal the wound herself. However, this is exactly what happens to many suffering with mental wounds. Because of the ignorance that surrounds mental illness, many suffer in silence for fear of being stigmatized and rejected.

Johann Weyer made a very powerful statement in the sixteenth century, "The mind like the body is susceptible to illness" (Comer, 2013). His point … if one's heart (the organ) needs assistance, if an arm is broken and requires setting, if one could lose sight or hearing and require professional help and there isn't something inherently wrong with the person or the act of seeking help, why then are those suffering from some sort of mental difficulty treated as if they are wrong or have done something wrong. It is very important that society come to terms with this notion that mental illness is akin to physical illness. The former does not lessen a person's worth, nor is the illness necessarily their fault.

"The mind, just like the body is susceptible to illness" … Johann Weyer

THINKING ABOUT YOUR THINKING – METACOGNITION

All of us have ongoing internal conversations. We have automatic thoughts that occur in particular situations. I refer to those automatic thoughts as one's internal tape recorder. For instance, imagine you are in a grocery store, it is time to check out and the line is extremely long. What happens upon seeing the long line? You have an automatic thought. What is it? Are you aware of this action automatically occurring within you thousands times over throughout a course of a day. Unless you are introspectively gifted or have engaged in self-awareness activities, it is unlikely that you have been taught to think about your thinking. Awareness of your thoughts is a very important state to achieve on this journey of self-love. And, particularly important to this process of exploration.

Note of Importance:

The automatic thought which occurred at the sight of the long line is either beneficial or costly. It is NOT neutral.

Our thoughts affect us in one way or another. This understanding is vital because what we think about ourselves is what we will be. Henry Ford famously stated: "Whether you think you can or think you can't, you're right." The Holy Scriptures says it this way: "As a man thinketh in his heart, so is he" Proverb 23:7. Napoleon Hill says, "Whatever you think today becomes what you are tomorrow." These perspectives highlight the power of our thoughts.

As such, tuning into our thoughts is an absolute must in order to fortify those thoughts which lend themselves toward betterment and our reducing self-limiting thinking patterns.

TRAINING YOURSELF TO TUNE IN

You can train yourself to become keenly aware of your thoughts by tuning into them, listening to your self-talk. Let's practice now. While reading these lines, what are you thinking? (Write your thoughts in the margin of the book). Perhaps you are saying to yourself (thinking), "this is nonsense, a waste of time," or "yes I know, I learned this in my psychology class," or maybe you are simply saying "I've not given much thought to my thinking." Whatever your thought is in this moment, know that it has power to affect your present and future.

If this is not a familiar act, thinking about your thinking may initially require considerable effort – commitment and perseverance. It can be downright exhausting. Nevertheless, I encourage you to practice this way of being. Again, this is an important step in the process of increasing self-love. Consider this: a steady diet of negative self-talk leads to self-depreciation. Mostly, life hindering self-talk continues because of lack of knowledge.

Many are simply unaware of their own internal conversations. Reflect on the following scenario:

A business owner (Kim) is told he will have to pitch his idea before the board of directors of a funding source in order to have his very important proposal considered. For some, this requirement would not pose a problem. However, for this entrepreneur a public speaking requirement is the worst possible of requests. Kim is not good at public speaking. In fact, he is terrified by the idea of having to complete this task. His immediate thought is to have an assistant complete the task on his behalf. This idea is short lived as Kim learns that consideration of a proposal is only granted if the company's owner does the presentation. One of two situations is likely to occur:

- The business owner cannot stand before anyone and intelligently talk about his product, especially those viewed as his superiors. His present self-talk hinders him, with messages like, "this is going to be a disaster, I am going to make a fool of myself, I will never remember what to say, they are going to hate my idea." Or, to take a line from Hollywood, "they're going to laugh at me." Failure is a likely outcome if the business owner never learns to think about the automatic conversations he has with himself, and take control by changing them.
- A successful pitch doesn't ignore that fact that Kim is terrified of public speaking. In fact, the likelihood of success is increased by an understanding of his terror. In this scenario Kim has done his homework. He has chosen to become fully aware of his internal conversation (tape recordings) when faced with public speaking. This awareness informs him of the need to change. Because he is now armed with the awareness that negative, self-limiting messages will stop him from achieving, his goal of acquiring adequate funding is achieved.

Now that Kim is self-aware, he is positioned to do something about it. What can he do? KIM CAN CHOOSE TO CHANGE HIS INTERNAL MESSAGE. Instead of saying, "this is going to be a disaster," Kim can learn to tell himself "this is going to be a challenge, but I have handled challenges in the past and can, therefore, handle this challenge." Instead of rehearsing negative self-statements, he can replace them with more beneficial, functional statements. "I am going to make a fool of myself" or "I will never remember what to say," can become, "I am going to do my very best, and that will have to be enough." Rather than stating, "they are going to hate my idea," Kim can gain knowledge and acquire tools that allow him to be okay with both successes and failures. He can arrive at a mental place that says "I don't know if the board of directors will accept or reject my idea, either way, however, I am going to move forward and it will be all right."

This story about Kim may appear to be a long-winded way of making my point. This is intentional as my goal is to paint a mental picture, *hopefully increasing the likelihood of understanding*, because the achievement of self-love is directly tied to what we tell ourselves.

What we think and that which we meditate on becomes who we are. Kody Bateman, in his book entitled *Promptings*, says it this way: "What we say subconsciously becomes our reality." It is that which materializes into our everyday existence. So if we are to continually become our better selves, we must (1) become aware of our internal thoughts by tuning into them, (2) determine whether the thoughts are beneficial or a hindrance to our goals, and (3) if a hindrance we MUST change the dialogue. If our thoughts are beneficial, we must fortify the dialogue. Stated in a not-so-scholarly way, "we must stop our stinkin', thinkin'."

I agree with Koty Bateman. It is important to learn to make the kind of self-statements that will lead to the achievement or increase of self-love. Here are some of the things I often tell myself:

> *I love me*
> *Kathy, you are a gift to others*
> *You make a positive difference in the lives of many*
> *God loves you*
> *I love life and it's loving me right back*
> *You are blessed to be loved by so many*

> *The world is better because you are in it*
> *You will achieve your life goals*
> *You will keep improving… bettering your best*
> *Kathy, you are all that and a bag of chips*

Koty Bateman calls these "I am" statements. Others refer to them as statements of affirmations or positive self-talk. I say it is the language of self-love. It's the type of conversation we learn to have with ourselves when we are experiencing self-love.

Please note, however, there needs to be balance.

This way of thinking and self-talk is not intended to promote dishonesty about our faults, errors, shortcomings, problematic behaviors and/or attitudes. Quite the contrary, learning to love ourselves requires full awareness of our entire being. Remember, this chapter is about self-exploration. As such, we explore ourselves in totality – the good, bad and ugly.

Along the lines of the bad and ugly, I make self-inquiries (judging how I am doing in life) with statements like:

> That wasn't the best choice, why did I do it?
> This is an unproductive, bad habit that needs to be changed.
> I was impatient with that person. I need to watch that behavior.
> Life is too short to spend all my time working and worrying.
> Kathy, you found yourself here again. What's going on? Why are you here again?

The caveat, however, is that as we embark on the path of self-love, we learn to avoid rehearsing that which will facilitates bondage, and choose to rehearse statements of personal liberation.

Robert Kiosaki says, "It's not what you say out of your mouth that determines your life, it's what you whisper to yourself that has the most power!" Too often we feel compelled to say what others expect us to say or what a particular situation demands (we feel the pressure of demand). When we believe or feel in this way, those positive, life-giving statements may be outwardly spoken but are not true reflections of our beliefs. To the degree that our internal (true) conversation doesn't match the externally spoken words, conflict ensues and is often followed by an inner conversational assault that goes something like this ...

> "Why did you lie? You keep doing the same thing even though it causes problems. You are fake! If people knew the real you, they would have nothing to do with you. You might as well just give up trying to be what you are not, you will never change. You are who you are, accept it. You are just like everyone else in your family, a loser."

An inner conversational assault can be very damaging to one's identity, emotions and state of mind, particularly if this is an ongoing occurrence.

We acknowledge self-talk that is a hindrance in order to work on changing it; yet we give energy to – rehearse, repeat, reinforce the internal dialogue that will better us. If continued, those statements will become a healthy diet of self-talk; increasing our likelihood of achieving increased levels of self-love.

Review

Learning to implement life-giving self-talk requires:

(1) rehearsing life-giving scenarios
(2) repeating life-giving words
(3) reinforcing life-giving behavior

BE INTENTIONAL ABOUT IDENTIFYING YOUR EVER CHANGING EMOTIONS

"An emotion is a complex psychological state that involves three distinct components: a subjective experience, a physiological response, and a behavioral or expressive response" (Hockenbury & Hockenbury, 2007).

(1) ***Subjective Experience*** – represents your unique way of experiencing a situation. Although we can have the same external experience, we very often have a different internal experience. It

23

is perception. We simply see things differently. This is because we have different backgrounds (*More about this later*).

(2) ***Physiological Response*** – represents your body's response. It may be stomach queasiness, rapid eye movement, racing heart, goose bumps, etc. These responses are often not visible to others.

(3) ***Behavioral or Expressive Response*** – represents what you do. For instance we generally smile when happy, frown and/or cry when sad and flee when afraid. These responses are always visible to others.

In our society, feelings or emotions are often viewed from a negative perspective: meaning, to operate from feelings represents weakness. You've probably heard or even spoken the term "oh she is just in her feelings," or "she's being emotional," or "well watch out, it's that time of the month." These types of statements shed a negative light on the feeling part of us.

If we are going to love ourselves better, we must not make emotions out to be the bad kid on the "human" block.

FEELINGS/EMOTIONS

I define feelings/emotions as "an inner spontaneous reaction to a person, place, thing or situation or the soul's response to life" (note: the first part of this statement comes from a *Marriage Encounters* participant booklet, and the second part comes from a student).

So let's do an exercise.

Make a two column list. At the top of one column write "good emotions" and at the top of the next column write "bad emotions," or use the one provided below. Now complete the list of good and bad emotions. There is no right or wrong number of emotions. Write as many on either side as you wish.

Good Emotions	Bad Emotions

Are you done? I am interested in knowing the type of list you've created. Feel free to share this with me at drkatherineejames@gmail.com or post on one of the *Dr. Katherine E. James* social media outlets before reading further.

While conducting workshops on emotions or teaching, I often utilize this exercise. The most common initial responses resemble the list below:

Good Emotions	Bad Emotions
Love	Hate
Joy/Happiness	Sadness
Trusting	Jealousy/Envy
Humility	Pride
Assurance	Fear
Peaceful	Anxious

Two realizations typically occur as the list develops: First, depending on the situation, the described emotions can be appropriately applied to either column. For instance, being joyful is good when one is rescued from a burning car. However, joy isn't an appropriate emotion when learning that someone has died in a burning car. Second, emotions are neither bad nor good, they just are.

As we go about our daily activities, in general, we don't plan to feel. We just feel. Typically this is what happens:

Our history + Current situation = Feelings

Our history – all experience (childhood, past relationships, employment, hopes, dreams, failures, accomplishments, etc.) that occurred in life prior to this current situation

Current situation – that which is happening now

Our history meets the current situation and we automatically feel (that is an inner spontaneous reaction). It is not planned, it simply is. What we feel makes sense, given who we are and all we have previously experienced. It is within this context that I reiterate feelings (not actions or behaviors) are neither good nor bad. They just are!

Although it isn't accurate to label feelings as good or bad, they can be accurately classified as beneficial or unbeneficial. For example, a history of being laughed at each time a child tried to recite a poem in elementary school is likely to develop fear of public speaking. The feeling of fear makes sense for this individual's history. However, 25 years later, and now an adult, this individual's job requires public speaking and she continues to be overtaken by fear. This feeling hinders her ability to be viewed as an asset to the employer. While the feeling makes sense (given the history), it is not beneficial but costly. The reason is because this very real feeling stops the employee from meeting the job demand.

Be Intentional about Identifying Your Ever Changing Emotions

There is hope! Emotions can be changed. Recognizing and labeling emotions is the first step toward changing them. Again, yes, as difficult as it may be to believe, we do have the power to change how we feel. We are *not* prisoner's of our emotions. The first step, however, is to recognize and honor our feelings as they currently are. Recognize simply means to honestly state the feeling as it actually is. Honor means to recognize that although the feeling may not be beneficial, it makes sense for who you are.

Emotions are a gift from God that can wreak havoc in our lives if they are not effectively managed. Effective management of feelings begins with identifying them. I submit, the average person is not attuned to her feelings. You say you don't believe me? Well put on your scientist or psychologist's hat and try this experiment. Go to five to ten people and begin talking about some current event, then ask them "how do you feel about the ...." Most people will undoubtedly tell you what they think, not how they feel. Unless an individual has been trained or is naturally gifted in this area, most are not skilled with identifying feelings (except for anger, this emotion is easily recognized). In fact, much of society frowns upon or is uncomfortable with discussions stemming from a "feeling" or emotional perspective. Some go as far to say that those of us who talk in this way are weak and illogical and that, we (according to the naysayers) are driven more by our emotions rather than by intellect.

In truth, it is the absence of feeling awareness or avoidance that increases the likelihood of personal weakness. Consider a couple that just can't seem to get beyond a particular argument.

The Thinking Approach

Each time they talk, the conversation is centered on what they think about the incident. They are giving their opinions, which continue to place them at opposite ends of the symbolic street. Now let's change the scenario and instead of the conversation centering on their thoughts, they focus on feelings. Originally the wife frequently communicated that it was not a good idea for the family to move to another state. Within the two months of receiving the news about the potential move, the wife's reasons grew from a few to dozens, as did the negative energy. The husband's approach was to state the facts of being able to grow in the company, increase pay and the experience of being in a new part of the country. This couple is at a stalemate and neither is sharing how they feel about the move.

The Feeling Approach

Now consider a feeling approach. Initially, the wife fails to share her fear of losing family and friend connections from which she receives tremendous physical and psychological support. She fears becoming overwhelmed by the responsibilities of being a wife, mom, and working outside of the home without her support system. Her husband, she believes, is being selfish and unreasonable, driven by money and his professional advancement desires: she shares this belief in a not so nice way. This gets her nowhere, being aggravated, she shouts I'm afraid to move. Now feelings have entered the picture and a new path of communication becomes available. In turn, the husband shares he too is afraid, but he is afraid of remaining and being unable to provide for his family, as he believes the company to be short lived in this region. However, he has assurances of lucrative opportunities in other states. Believe it or not, the shared fear is fertile ground; it is a commonplace from which to begin productive conversations.

In essence, it was the same emotion fueling the arguments and driving a wedge between the couple. Honesty about their feelings, in addition to their thoughts, increased avenues for dialogue. Think about it this way: it is much easier to dismiss someone's thought than it is to dismiss his or her feeling (especially if we learned the lesson that all feelings make sense from an historical perspective). When we begin to talk feelings with those we love, deeper level of connections are made possible. Think talk often blocks this level of intimacy. In this instance, the difference between thinking and feeling is paramount; one closes doors while the other not only opens, but creates new doors.

Identifying Feelings

In order to engage step one of identifying feelings, we must become familiar with *feeling language*. A simple Internet search will help. Look for "feeling wheels" or "feeling charts" and a world of feeling language will be opened to you. Begin practicing with tools of this kind as you learn or improve feeling identification. This is an important first step into the world of feelings. Since we have diminished power to change that which we have not accurately identified, let's put first things first and learn the language of our emotions.

As you make this life change, use each conversation as an opportunity to talk emotively. Instead of telling a person what you think, share with her how you feel and watch the conversation take on a different, yet exciting feel (no pun intended). In the beginning stages, this way of being is not easy-- but it is worth overcoming the challenge. Many people are uncomfortable talking in feeling terms. Some are terrified of the vulnerability inherent in this type of communication. Mostly, it is because it is a foreign way of being, they are simply not used to communicating in this way. Don't give up, though, because it's worth the effort.

Imagine the freedom of freely saying: "I hurt" "I am afraid" "I feel lost" "I am happy." We are more likely to give children permission to talk in these ways, but in many ways we tell adults to keep it to themselves. This liberating way of being is ours (adults) to have as well.

PAY ATTENTION TO YOUR PHYSICAL RESPONSES (INTERNAL AND EXTERNAL EXPERIENCES)

Perhaps you are asking what in the world am I talking about. Picture this: you are in a movie theatre watching a horror film and consequently you are frightened. What is your physical response? Fear reactions are well researched, categorized into the fight or flight responses - where one either prepares to stand her ground and face the threat, or flee for safety. Either way, there is a distinct physical response. Recall the horror film, physical responses likely included a racing heart, perspiration, and bulging eyes with dilated pupils, along with tensed muscles. Get the idea?

A similar response occurs when we have pleasant experiences. The heart rate increases, the stomach reacts (often referred to as butterflies), and pupils may dilate as our body responds in delight. Our physical body or physiological responses clue us into our feelings. If honored – paid attention to -- the physical response keep us honest. For instance, you may have convinced yourself that you are no longer bothered by the argument you previously had with your neighbor. However, if each time you see the neighbor your stomach responds in knots, or you have some other gut response, then the likelihood of you being over the argument is not likely at all. The probable truth is that you are still bothered and the concern is taking up mental space because the situation is not resolved. Reflecting on the previous meta-cognition discussion, thinking about the matter (conscious or unconscious) is holding you hostage in a state of being bothered. Perhaps you are asking: How do I stop my stomach from responding? You do this while keeping in mind that our internal and external experiences cue us into our feeling and thinking reality and, therefore, abetting that feeling in your stomach may seem impossible.

Part of the answer to stopping the physical response is found in our previous discussion: changing our internal conversation about the person and moving from a powerless to a powerful posture, if necessary. It may be true, your neighbor is not a nice person, life would be easier if he would simply cooperate or move. Yet he continues to be abrasive and unpleasant, even after being aware of his impact on others. *In light of this type of behavior, many would continue to focus on self-defeating statements such as: he is so irritating; I wish he would move, he's such a mean and horrible person; it's no wonder he's always alone, and I certainly wouldn't want to be his friend.* The problem with exerting energy in this direction is the absence of power. We simply have no power to change another person! But…*we can change ourselves.*

The place of power sounds like this: instead of allowing the neighbor's presence to lead to my stomach ache, I can practice self-empowering statements that will release me from my "bad neighbor bondage," my self-imposed prison. Try on some of these statements: *This is going to be a great day; I will be grateful today; I am thankful for life; all is not going as I desire it to, but I can work toward the necessary change; I am not happy today, but there is always tomorrow; things are tough now, but it won't always be this way.*

Along with speaking positive statements, in most cases, it is also important to speak the fact. This helps us avoid living in a fairytale like state. Life is real, and we have the ability to change, which often changes our situations.

There are many avenues to freedom from a self-imposed psychological bondage. Let me offer a well-known one at this juncture of our discussion. The Serenity Prayer: *God grant me the serenity to accept the things I cannot change, the courage to change the things I can, and the wisdom to know the difference.* Let's take a closer look. (Remember we are still discussing how to manage our physical responses: Who wants to walk around with a stomachache anyway?)

God grant me the serenity to accept the things I cannot change. **We have no power to change other people, even God gives them choice.**

The courage to change the things I can ... **We can change ourselves, but often it requires bravery, because a prerequisite to intentional change is an investigation into what needs to be changed. For some, facing ourselves is the scariest of all endeavors. It may seem easier to blame others for our current problem than be honest with ourselves.**

And the wisdom to know the difference. **We have power of change only over ourselves and not others. Forcing or manipulating others into doing as we desire doesn't change them; it is called coercion, strong-arming, bullying, applying pressure, oppression – you get the point.**

Listen to your body; strong physical responses – racing heart, tensed muscles, stomach flutters or aches are physical clues of your emotions and thoughts. Don't ignore them!

The next time you recognize a strong physical response, representing some type of psychological bondage, apply the serenity prayer. Even if you don't believe in God, the principle still works. You are acknowledging and asserting the need to: accept the things you cannot change, the need for courage to change what you can, and the need for wisdom to distinguish between the two.

ENGAGE IN ACTIVITIES THAT WILL INCREASE YOUR RELATIONAL AWARENESS

This, too, requires courage. Unfortunately, American society appears to celebrate appearance rather than substance. It's the idea that something only has to look good; there is little requirement for it to actually *be* good. This isn't a factual statement, certainly not as it pertains to healthy living. An apple that looks good, but is rotten to the core, is not edible and, therefore, not good or beneficial. So what's my point? Most relationships remain at the surface level. As a rule, people are not invited to go beyond our "peeling layer." To take it further, they certainly are not invited to inform us of the impact of our inner state of being. Do others experience a primarily fresh, life-giving experience when engaging us? Or do they experience a tainted, rotten core experience when engaging us? Again, most don't invite others into their lives to engage in assessment activities.

Some may not see this as a problem. However, it is a problem when those in a relationship are not able or willing to tell one another the truth. Have you ever experienced someone describing herself to be a certain way and you are thinking: "Who you?" Or, have you listened to a person discuss her strong dislike for someone because of a particular trait, while this same individual is unable or unwilling to see that same behavior operating in her life? This is when we make sarcastic statements like, "Boy isn't *this* the pot calling the kettle black."

Because of how our society typically functions on a surface or appearance level, it is more likely that we Americans do not actively invite others to tell us the truth about their experiences with us. This behavior generally leaves many without an understanding of their impact on others. Thus, people often believe themselves to affect others in a particular way, but have not inquired to test this belief. Basically, few ask others "how do I impact you?" If others don't tell us, then we assume – for better or worse.

All is not lost. There are many ways to increase relational awareness:

1. **Conversation**: Have a conversation with a trusted friend or family member. Give this person permission to be totally honest about his or her experiences and observations of you. Remember, however, this is often an uncomfortable and perhaps risky endeavor for both of you. You may not want to hear what will be said (the truth, when we are not used to hearing it, can be difficult to hear). After hearing the truth, you may be tempted to treat the person differently. There is potential loss for the both of you by engaging in honesty. However, I believe it is worth the risk.

   Too often, we continue to experience the same behavioral hindrances because we remain ignorant to their presence and the impact they have on our life and those with whom we engage. There is a way out of this unproductive way of being, which takes us back to the opening sentence of this section. Give a trusted family member or friend permission to be honest with you about your impact on others. Once you receive this valuable information, make the necessary adjustment to change. Also, be careful how you treat this person after she has shared. Do not punish her for telling you the truth about you, as she sees it.

2. **Listen to others**: Carefully listen to the words others use to describe you. A question to ask: what is my most noticeable personality characteristic? How would those I consistently engage answer this question? It is important to avoid dismissing what others have to

say about us. Particularly, when we hear others repeatedly describe us in a similar fashion, it's worth some consideration. At the very least, when multiple people are having the same experience, there is some level of validity to their descriptions, whether or not their experience was your intended outcome. If the descriptions are favorable to healthy living, fortify the behavior. If they are unfavorable to healthy living, begin the process of behavioral modification - change it.

3. **Exercises**: There are many exercises available that aid in gaining insight into one's personality traits. The following exercise helps with understanding one's personality traits by showing how others experience us:

The Johari Window can be found through a simple Internet search.

This personality inventory was invented by Joseph Luft and Harrington Ingham in the 1950s as a model for mapping personality awareness. From a list of adjectives, select those that apply, then ask others to select descriptors of you from the same list. These activities are followed up by a grid comparing the overlapping and divergent selections.

Other self-awareness tools include: varying types of personality inventories, spiritual gifts assessments, journaling, and skills assessments – just to name a few.

ABOUT ME ... SELF-EXPLORATION

Often I find myself asking these questions: Kathy, why did you do (think) that? So, what was that response about? What are you feeling? What do you need? Do you realize that you act this way when you are afraid? Self-inquiry continually keeps me aware of my inner ways of being – why I act, feel, believe, and think as I do.

Additionally, I have wonderful people in my life who speak the truth to me about me. They hold me accountable to my declared values and beliefs.

I pay attention to how I impact others. Do others leave me whole? Have I given out or taken? Are others better off for having been in my company or did it cost them? Bearing in mind how we impact others provides us with additional insight.

Finally, when assessing my impact on others, I often consider the outcome of the encounter. Was I added value?

OPPORTUNITY FOR REFLECTIONS

CHAPTER THREE

SELF-DISCOVERY

Man cannot love that which he does not know.

- James Allen

Self-discovery is the state of becoming fully aware of your current state of being and doing – discovering who you are now. It is a sober look at our current self, not a false self who we present ourselves to be, or who we hope or plan to be in the future. Neither is it our capitulation to who others demand us to be. This self-discovery journey is about coming to know who we ARE, right now.

Ask yourself the obvious question: Who am I? You may say, well this is a stupid question. Of course I know who I am. Wonderful! I say to that. Perhaps you may feel the need to skip this chapter and, if so, that is certainly your right. Before you do, however, consider the possibility that you may discover (no pun intended) something that may be beneficial for others, if not for you. So go ahead, if for no other reason but to prove me wrong, read the entire chapter.

Let's discover…

The previous chapter led you into the self-discovery territory. Discovery is a natural outgrowth of exploration; exploration brings with it the notion of traveling and seeking, while finding is the essence of the discovery process.

Courage is required to move forward in this portion of the book. Particularly when we are not accustomed to engaging in self "findings."

This leg of the journey can be quite tumultuous. Some expend substantial energy hiding from self; avoiding conversations, readings, stimuli that would lead one into an internal investigation. As we look at ourselves and discover the positive aspectss--being loving, hospitable, and organized, for example-- the journey is not so challenging. Contrastingly, when the journey reveals behaviors that are not so pretty, like being short tempered, selfish, manipulative or lazy, the likelihood of hiding (even from ourselves) is increased.

This is an important step toward removing the masks that we wear to self-protect. When speaking of wearing masks, the conversation often deals with notions of hiding from others. However, before we make the choice to hide from others, we have likely made the choice to hide some element from our self. In this moment you are being asked to consider the idea of removing the mask that hides you from you. It may be necessary to take it slow, or stated another way, take baby steps.

NOTE of caution:

If you have exerted substantial energy suppressing some element of your personality or behavior, there is a good chance it is too painful for you to face alone. As a therapist, it would be unethical of me if I neglected to caution you of the potential need to seek professional help during this process. Basically, if this description of substantial hiding resembles your behavior, you have probably engaged a coping or ego defense mechanism to avoid being bombarded by your ego. As long as this process doesn't hinder one from fully living, employing ego-defense mechanisms is a healthy dynamic. However, for most of us there comes a time in life when the long engaged coping mechanisms are more costly than beneficial.

What I most want you to hear now is this: If this exercise becomes too overwhelming or painful, *don't do it alone.* Either invite someone you know to walk with you on this portion of the journey, or seek professional help. But *do not* take the following steps alone.

STEPS OF DISCOVERY

There are many paths to what I have termed as "self-findings." Let me suggest a few that have been found to be helpful.

1. **Be honest with yourself**: we know ourselves better than anyone else. Regardless of how challenging it may be to acknowledge some flaw, shortcoming or limitation in our behavior, it is necessary to be completely honest with ourselves about them.

   Practice honesty (whether good or bad, be honest)

   Here is an example:

   Untruth: "I am good at listening to others"

   Truth: "I'm not good at listening, I'm good at appearing to be a good listener; actually I don't really care what others are talking about unless they are talking about me or something that interests me."

2. **Make a "Self Findings" list**: again lists are very important. In a way they help to keep us honest by placing reality before us in written form. What did you discover about your feelings? What did you discover about your behavior or thoughts? Write your findings and appropriately categorize them. For example, you may have a list that reads, "I feel good about," "I don't feel good about," "This behavior benefits me," "Need to change that thought." You decide the type of list that works for you. The primary goal is discovery and awareness.

   Additional questions to ask: (1) Do I often act incongruently – what I feel on the inside does not match what I show on the outside - out of pressure and fear, (2) Am I so concerned about others' opinions of me that I pretend to be what I am not? (3) How do I desire to be in the future? Do I pretend to be that now?

3. **Impact**: consider how you impact your environment. A first step is discovering how we behave, think and feel. The next step involves understanding how our way of being (behavior, thoughts and feelings) impacts others and ourselves. Next, ask yourself is the impact of your predominant way of being a life-enhancing or life-hindering behavior; if it isn't life-enhancing for you then it isn't for others either. If it is life-enhancing for others, chances are that it is life-enhancing for you as well. Sowing and reaping, what goes around comes around and karma all speak to the importance of how we interact with self and others. In all we do, we are sowing seeds and we will get a return – for better or worse.

Make sure the impact you have on yourself and others is such that you welcome the return from your past behavior. We can often fool others about those aspects of our lives we wish to keep secret. We can ignore certain realities about ourselves, choosing to remain in the dark. Or, we can take the journey of self-discovery and come to know ourselves better. There is inherent power in knowledge, in knowing.

About Me ... Self-Discovery

As previously stated, there is ongoing discussion occurring within me. As I find myself in situations, I identify what is going on internally and make inquiries like: Why am I like this? Why am I feeling this way? What do I want in this situation? Am I truly being myself now? What am I afraid of, why am I tempted to hide, to self-protect right now? What do I believe is at stake? What draws me toward this person? How does this person repel me? It is a never- ending internal conversation that at times becomes a bit too much. Why am I this way? I have no definitive answer.

This area of life came with maturity. I don't have any childhood stories to depict self-discovery, but many from my adulthood. One hot summer day I was preparing to attend a ceremony to honor graduating students. I found myself in front of a mirror attempting to press the roots of my hair because they had grown out from my perm in preparation for going into locs. If you know anything about thick, coarse African American hair, you understand I was not in a good situation. To add insult to injury, I perspire easily.

Here is the picture: (1) I am running late for the event, (2) attempting to do my own hair as I failed to get to the beauty salon, (3) while running a hot pressing comb through my edges in order to match the remainder of my straight permed hair, I am wearing a very hot lined linen suit.

Can you imagine the internal conversation occurring at this moment? Why did you wait so late to get started? You are going to be late. You have got to get better at time management. If you didn't procrastinate so much your hair would be done and you wouldn't be trying to straighten your hair in 90-degree weather. In the midst of all the internal madness, I had an epiphany and made the following statement: "In all of your years of living combined, you have not put this much energy into your hair. Why are you doing so now? What is different about this situation that you are feeling a need to be other than who you are? What do you believe is at stake? What's important?

Answers to all these questions fit within two responses: (1) It does matter that I look presentable and mixed match hair wasn't acceptable so I was attempting to rectify this situation, and (2) my tendency to procrastinate got me into this situation, not a need to people-please or present myself in some in-authentic way. I was able to arrive at these two answers through my ongoing practice of exploration and discovery. See above *#1 Be honest with yourself.*

After the epiphany I repeated the statement, "In all your years of living combined, you have not put this much energy into your hair." I continued with the following concluding statement, "and you are not about to start now." At that very moment I decided to cut off all of the permed hair and wear a short afro until such time that there was enough length to begin the locing process.

It was this practice of internally conversing that led to the discovery of why I was in this predicament, positioning me to make better choices in the future.

OPPORTUNITY FOR REFLECTIONS

CHAPTER FOUR

SELF-ACCEPTANCE

The greatest trap in our life is not success, popularity or power, but self-rejection.
- Henri Nouwen

Self-acceptance is my refusal to be in an adversarial relationship with myself.
- Nathaniel Brand

Self-acceptance is a sobering acknowledgment of our current selves. It says … I know who I am. I am clear about my strengths and my weaknesses. I recognize my accomplishments and failures. I know my limitations and my abilities. I am intimate with all that I currently am – my fears, aspirations, hopes, dreams, beliefs, doubts, likes, dislikes, irritations, and biases. I am unaware of my blind spots, but in pursuit of uncovering those as well. This type of awareness is at odds with masking, pretense, hiding or engaging in chameleon-like behavior. In essence, there is acceptance of the good, bad, ugly and indifferent parts of us. Self-acceptance, says "it is what it is." From this perspective I am free to be me without apology to self or others. Ultimately, acceptance allows me to be okay with all of me.

Introduced in this chapter is the concept of "BE", representing *being psychologically, emotionally, and relationally authentic*. While in this state, you are comfortable with your current state of being. There is no compelling need of pretense, to act in ways that are incongruent with your thoughts and feelings. As situations are presented you respond authentically to them. Self-acceptance gives you permission to be authentically you in every situation. I once heard authenticity explained in this way: "Your inners and outers Match."

Note of Caution: Authenticity is not a license to mistreat others. Statements such as, "well this is just the way I am," "I'm only being honest," "Honesty is the best policy," are often pronouncements intended to justify acts of rudeness, inconsideration, abrasiveness or meanness. This way of being is not loving behavior. Self-acceptance is never intended to lead to the rejection of others. In fact, the opposite is expected since a natural outgrowth of love for self is the increased capacity to love others. I am not saying that relationships are not affected by increased levels of authenticity. Indeed they are. The impact, however, ought *not* to be that which is relationally destructive, but instead enhancing. Self-acceptance, in a sense, is letting ourselves off the hook, an extension of mercy for our ways that haven't been life-giving. As we grow in grace for self, we have increased capacity to extend grace to others.

Whereas authenticity is not a license to mistreat others, it does bring a responsibility to speak the truth in love. Living authentically compels us to speak truth for the betterment of self and others. In this place, one does not use her newfound freedom to tear others down, under the guise of "I'm just speaking the truth." Living authentically is a liberating, not terrorizing state of being. The following poem captures my sentiment on the subject:

Taken from "Miscellaneous Poems," by Mary Ann Pietzker, published in 1872 by Griffith and Farran of London (at the "corner of St. Paul's Churchyard").

"Is It True? Is It Necessary? Is It Kind?

Oh! Stay, dear child, one moment stay,
Before a word you speak,
That can do harm in any way
To the poor, or to the weak;
And never say of any one
What you'd not have said of you,
Ere you ask yourself the question,
"Is the accusation true?"

And if 'tis true, for I suppose
You would not tell a lie;
Before the failings you expose
Of friend or enemy:
Yet even then be careful, very;
Pause and your words well weigh,
And ask if it be necessary,
What you're about to say.

And should it necessary be,
At least you deem it so,
Yet speak not unadvisedly
Of friend or even foe,
Till in your secret soul you seek
For some excuse to find;
And ere the thoughtless word you speak,
Ask yourself, "Is it kind?"

When you have ask'd these questions three—
True,—Necessary,—Kind,—
Ask'd them in all sincerity,
I think that you will find,
It is not hardship to obey
The command of our Blessed Lord,—
No ill of any man to say;
No, not a single word.

A final word on this: "sticks and stones will break my bones but words will never hurt me." This has been told to many children and subsequently recited by them. But, this is an inaccurate statement and belief in it the cause of much, much harm. Read some of the domestic violence literature and you will discover that words are sometimes more damaging than broken bones. Bones mend, but soul-destructive words may take a lifetime to mend.

About Me ... My Journey of Authenticity and Self-Acceptance

Of course I didn't come into this world with my current level of authenticity. As a child, I, like countless others, learned very early on the benefits of hiding my true self (feelings, thoughts, desires, disappointments, etc.) – ways of self-protecting. Today, I clearly understand what I lacked the capacity to know as a child: this type of behavior becomes more costly as one matures. A life of masking (hiding) comes at a high cost. At the very least it hinders us from being and showing our true selves and impedes the way for authentic encounters with others.

In middle school some teens were beginning to experiment with drinking and sex. I vividly recall two invitations that, if accepted, had the capacity to greatly alter the trajectory of my young life. First, came the offer to join the crowd in the consumption of an alcoholic beverage. I remember thinking that I wanted no part of this as I had seen my share of alcohol consumption in my own family. So I refused. The next offer came in the way of a challenge as a group of girls was tallying who had and had not engaged in sexual activities. It was obvious since they all claimed to be amongst those who had, that those who had not were going to be in for some unpleasant treatment.

At this point, I made one of the best decisions of my young life, to be okay with being different. The decision required me to be authentic and tell the truth about my sexual encounters to date – no matter how unpopular my position, the reality was sexual encounters were nonexistent in my life. Resultantly, I gained the stigmatizing label of "virgin." What these young girls could not have known is that my stubbornness (unwillingness to be bullied) would lead me to proudly wear the label as a badge instead of in shame. This posture set a stage for my increased ability to be comfortable with nonconformity. I learned through these and countless other similar incidences, that not only was it okay to be different, but it was often better. I continually stood out from the crowd. I was special, not less than, because I was different. As I practiced being authentic, it became increasingly easier for me to accept me – the good, bad, and ugly parts.

Today, self-acceptance is as common to me as breathing. I know my strengths and weaknesses, am aware of my accomplishments and failures, understand my limitations and my abilities. I am intimate with most of who I currently am – fears, aspirations, hopes, dreams, beliefs, doubts, likes, dislikes, irritations, and biases. I am unaware of blind spots, but always in pursuit of revelation in these areas of my life. To that end, I know myself very well and yet... *I accept all of me.* I refuse to wear masks and pretend to be other than who I am. I will not pay the price of pretense, it cost way too much. Confidence, esteem, satisfaction and inner peace are all at risk when we wear a mask more often than not.

Hopefully you have noticed at no time have I used the word rejection in relation to me. This is because I reject no part of me. The ways of being, doing or thinking that are not beneficial to healthy living are not rejected but identified, accepted and put in the coffer of change. Some may say this is a play on words, that both words "reject" and "change" is the same in this situation. They may be. However, I believe you would agree with me, saying I change my mind sounds a lot better than saying I reject my mind. You see, when put that way the difference becomes tangible. I am free to change all parts of me that are not profitable for healthy living. However, I am never free to reject any part of me.

An area of my life where I often attempt to change, but to date have fallen short, is weight. I distinctly recall the summer when I went from wearing a girl's 14 to a woman's 10/12. Some may say that's impossible, but it really happened. By the time I went back to school (middle school) I was well on my way to a 14. Certainly by the time I entered high-school the next year, I was a solid 14 while a majority of my peers average sizes 7/8 or 9/10. Today, as I put the final touches on this book, I am at my heaviest (a size 26 and just over 300 pounds). For most of my adult life, since the birth of my son – only 28 years ago – I have averaged at size 24.

I know how to lose weight, as I have loss substantial weight many times after arriving at my first size 24. But I have yet to conquer maintenance – how to keep the darn weight off; how not to return to old patterns that help to maintain this size. Not lost on me are the inherent risks of being an overweight African American woman (diabetes, hypertension, heart disease). To date, I've not experienced any of these, and I am believing that I won't. Towards this goal, I have adopted the slogan "Never Quit Quitting." This means I will never give in to being overweight because it is simply not the healthiest way of being. So I generally walk two to three miles daily in the summer and adjust my eating to help take the weight off. I'm less focused in the winter months, but try to incorporate some movement.

If someone has a remedy, please enlighten me. Here is part of what I've heard others say about those of us who are overweight:

"IT'S LAZINESS"

Well, I work three jobs, own my own business, am very active in my church, rarely miss important functions (graduations, weddings, showers, cheerleading competitions, proms, birthday celebrations, hospital visitations, pledge crossings, impromptu drop ins to say I'm thinking about you, community engagements, etc.).

"YOU JUST NEED TO MAKE UP YOUR MIND"

I have made up my mind to lose weight many times and while I am in the state, I am very diligent and focused. The problem I've experienced is that I am unable to keep a made up mind.

"IF THE DOCTOR TELLS YOU TO LOSE WEIGHT ..."

Well, seeing the word obese on one's medical charts is certainly a shock the first time. It doesn't feel good and it is temporary motivation. But, I eventually "fall off the wagon again."

Again, I will never quit quitting.

I sometimes joke about one downfall of having high self-esteem is self-acceptance, meaning that others' negative opinion about my weight doesn't move me one way or the other. I can't be shamed into losing weight. I certainly need to lose weight, but not for appearance sake – to fit society's definition of beauty, but to be healthy that I can remain on earth a little longer. For without a doubt, I am beautiful just as I am (inside and out).

NOTE: *It's quite okay to say nice things about yourself; doing so doesn't mean you are conceited, it simply means that you are for you.*

My main point is this: being overweight in NO WAY changes my value – I am as valuable as anyone, even those half my size. Although I would like to be smaller, I wouldn't love myself more if I were smaller. When I look in the mirror now, I love the woman who looks back at me. When I finally lose and keep this weight off, I will look in the mirror and love me more. However, this increased love will not be because I have lost the weight, but because I have continued to do my self-love work. As long as I do the work, I will learn to love me better, whether that is at 300 plus pounds or somewhere around my goal weight of 185 lbs.

Don't forget about the note of caution - *authenticity is not a license to mistreat others.* Heeding this warning will help to maintain the needed balance of love for self and others as you progress on this journey.

OPPORTUNITY FOR REFLECTIONS

CHAPTER FIVE

SELF-FORGIVENESS

If we really want to love, we must learn how to forgive.

- Mother Theresa

You will begin to heal when you let go of past hurts, forgive those who have wronged you and learn to forgive yourself for your mistakes.

– Author Unknown

So what is this notion of forgiveness? Synonyms for forgiveness are to pardon, give clemency, to exonerate, give amnesty or mercy. Let me be the first to say, you have a right to forgive yourself. From the Holy Scriptures, the Apostle Paul said, "All have sinned and fallen short of the glory of God" (Romans 3:23). There is no perfect person on this earth. We have all made mistakes. Perhaps we have let people down, or made horrible statements to or about people. Maybe we cheated in some way, or failed to live up to own moral code. We may even have been instrumental in someone being physically harmed or in the loss of life. This list could go on and on. The point I am making, in order to achieve self-love, you must release yourself of the penalty of unforgiveness exacted for the offense. You must free yourself and walk out of the self, or others', imposed prison.

Maybe at this point you are saying, "But you don't know what I have done." No I don't. Or you may believe you don't deserve to be forgiven. Perhaps, your experience is that others (who you love and value) like your mother, father, sibling, spouse, child or friend, have not forgiven you and you believe this bondage to be warranted. It is not my place to judge, it doesn't matter to me. Because accepting any of those reasons (as valid as they may seem) means that you will remain in an unforgiven state. And I am not willing to accept that, because forgiving yourself and others is too important to accept any reason or excuse for not doing so. What does matter, however, is your ability to soberly face your offense; call it what it is (cheating, lying, harming, neglecting) and take the power back from it. The reality here is, until you do so, you have locked yourself into a psychological, emotional and spiritual prison that is (according to research) also negatively affecting your body and robbing you of your best possible life. You have to face it and eventually let it go!

So the next logical question is how? Actually, it is a simple four-step process. Simple, however, isn't necessarily easy. Many factors determine the ease or difficulty in which you are able to engage these steps. No matter where you fall on the continuum, remember, you have a right to forgive yourself.

First step – Acknowledgment

Acknowledge the offense for what it is. Don't sugar coat it, or magnify it. Be as accurate as possible about your role in the offense and it's magnitude in the grand scheme of things.

Second step – Admittance

Admit how the offense has affected you and others. Again, be completely honest. Avoid exaggerating or diminishing the reality.

Third step – Statement of Forgiveness

State what you forgive yourself of, what you release yourself from and how you expect life to be different after accepting forgiveness.

Fourth step – Celebrate

Celebrate your release from bondage. It may take time to get to the point of celebration. Also, it may be helpful to remember this step is not about celebrating the offense, but about the celebration of self-forgiveness for whatever your role was in the offense – thereby releasing yourself from bondage. Again, this step is paramount in your process so don't skip it.

NOTE: You may need to repeat these steps until you fully achieve self-forgiveness. I encourage you to avoid skipping a step. The cyclical and orderly process of each step is designed with a particular purpose in mind.

Let's take a look at specific scenarios.

HARM WE'VE CAUSED OTHERS

The forgiveness portion, unlike other sections of this book, may involve another person. There are times when releasing ourselves requires making amends with others. CAUTION: This is not an act of you seeking forgiveness from someone; remember, you are giving yourself the gift of forgiveness, an act not contingent upon the response of another. However, part of our letting go and moving beyond our self-imposed prison may require going to another, owning up to our part and apologizing for particular actions or lack of actions. You alone can make the determination as to whether or not this step of involving others is necessary.

Why do this? Why possibly open the door to further hurt and pain? The Holy Scriptures requires reconciliation where possible. According to Mathew 5:23, we are to be reconciled to our brothers. Romans 12:18 require that we live peaceable with all men as it relates to the part that we play in the matter. It may not be possible, timely or expedient to approach the person offended by you. If this is the situation, move on in your journey and diligently work toward forgiving yourself. However, when it is possible, timely and expedient don't allow anything to stop you from engaging in this act of courage. Give the gift and set yourself free!

When our acts have left others wounded - we have left a trail of hurt, disappointment, disillusionment, pain and/or suffering - the need to apologize, express sorrow for past behavior may be necessary to move on.

Remember, others may not forgive you. They may believe you should never be forgiven, that you should pay for the offense for the remainder of your life. This state of belief often leads to their bondage; it doesn't have to lead to yours as well. Additionally, your choice of freedom is not their decision to make, it is yours. Actively expressing sorrow for your prior behavior is simply another act of cleansing, done only if necessary. When necessary and possible, we muster up the needed attitude (courage, sorrow, repentance) and go about the act of expressing sorrow. Perhaps, contacting the person is no longer a possibility. She may have moved away and is no longer in communication, or even deceased. However, releasing yourself, even in the person's absence, is still an option. I believe this act to be a prerequisite to self-forgiveness. The counseling field offers options.

One particular exercise is called the empty chair and is espoused by Gestalt Therapy. The technique requires the actual use of an empty chair where you sit before the empty chair, visualizes the person sitting before you, then you proceed with the apology. This technique has been instrumental in bringing about emotional release, similar to that which often occurs when done in the presence of an actual person. [**Please *do not* attempt these counseling techniques without the help of a professional mental health practitioner! They are mentioned here to provide an example of possible exercises, not as an invitation to try alone.**]

Either way, in person, over the phone, through the use of other technologies, or from the empty chair perspective, it's time to move forward on the journey of obtaining or increasing self-love by making the necessary amends through apology – expressing sorrow.

HARM OTHERS HAVE CAUSED US OR HARM WE HAVE CAUSED OURSELVES

When others have caused us harm, it may be necessary to offer ourselves forgiveness for the role we played in this. Perhaps, it was a parent who caused the harm, or some other family member. It could have been a spouse or trusted friend. Maybe it was a coworker, acquaintance or even a stranger. The often-erroneous and sometimes accurate thought is we allowed them to take advantage of us, to embarrass us, or to abuse us in some way (physical, mental, sexual). Ultimately, we understand that harm was caused and we didn't manage to stop it from occurring. So is it our fault? We may be fully at fault or hold no responsibility at all for the harm.

Sometimes it isn't others we need to forgive, but ourselves. From time to time we are reminded of our mistakes and misguided choices. We may be able to recall times when our (not other's) choices placed us in harm's way. Considerations of these past choices and consequences often bring sorrow, despair, exacerbation, regret or even hopelessness. Again, so is it our fault? Perhaps, perhaps not. Either way, we are now faced with the choice of achieving or increasing self-love. An unknown author stated, *"You will begin to heal when you let go of past hurts, forgive those who have wronged you, and learn to forgive yourself for your mistakes."* Again this is a choice, you and I will need to let go, to release ourselves of blame from the role we played in the harm that others caused us, or the harm inflicted on ourselves.

A way of engaging in self-injurious behavior is beating ourselves up for that which we had no control over. We are never at fault for the choices others have made, even when those choices led to our harm. To continue to blame ourselves for the harm others inflicted on us gives them power and keeps us imprisoned.

I am about to make a statement (shared by a beloved mentor – Dr. David Abbott – who is no longer with us) and am sure that I will repeat it before the book's end, because I believe it to be a psychologically life-giving posture.

"At any given time, people are doing the best they know to do."

What do you think about this statement? Many are at odds with it, because in our mind's eye we can recount numerous situations where, upon assessment of someone's behavior we draw the conclusion that they knew better and therefore should or could have done better. Generally, with this statement comes judgment of behavior and in some cases there is an expectation of recompense. When we function from the posture that they knew better, we expect others to act in a way that we demand and deem appropriate. When they fail to act in expected ways we are disturbed. Why? Because (according to our assessment) they know better and, therefore, ought to have done better.

As I have matured in life, I have opted to assume the psychological posture that "at any given time, people are doing the best they know to do and when they know better they do better." The knowing I refer to is not simply speaking of an intellectual attainment of a matter. I am also referencing the acceptance or owning of it. Think about it this way: a person has been told and comprehends that telling the truth is the right thing to do. And yet, the person finds that lying works for her. This individual will continue to tell lies until she comes to know the value of truth from a heart, instead of a head-only, perspective. It is then that she truly "knows" better. At this point of knowing, truth opposed to lying has become a part of her – a preferred way of being, not merely something that she thinks about, but it is now a part of who she is.

That explanation was a long way of saying let yourself off the hook for that which you didn't know at the time of allowing others to harm you; or you harming yourself. Perhaps you now truly know (have owned it) better and will subsequently do better.

Here's another example. How many of us know (intellectually) that undisciplined credit card use is problematic and yet we continue to use them – especially around Christmas time. Then at some point in life it clicks, we have that epiphany or "ah ha" moment; we come to understand the bondage and risks that comes with undisciplined spending. Is it that we didn't know better before the awakening? Certainly we did. We understood the liability that accompanies spending more money than we have to spend. We felt the stress and pressure that came along with the credit balances and reminders of our poor choices. We understood that the behavior would lead us into further bondage. But we understood it from an intellectual, rather than heart driven perspective. Subsequently, we didn't do better.

If we are to move forward in wellness, we need both. We need to comprehend matters of life from a thinking perspective and we need to know them at a deeper level, at a heart level.

NOTE OF CAUTION: There are times when one's behavior is so self (or other) destructive there isn't time to psychologically ascend to this place of knowing; the behavior is so costly, it simply must cease. Individuals engaging at this level don't know (heart perspective) better and thus will not do better. Unfortunately, in these situations, the involvement of external authoritative forces like parents, authority figures or even law enforcement is often required. It is far better to police our own selves (our behavior), than to be policed by others.

Psychologically healthy people protect themselves from those who have yet to do better because they have not come to *know* better. Another statement that powerfully informs me is "when people show you who they are, believe them." I only heard this statement about four years ago, but it so resonated with the way I engage people, that I have incorporated it into my repertoire for understanding others.

About Me ... Responding to Others For Who They Are Instead Of Who I Demand Them To Be?

At family gatherings, I noticed continued complaints about particular family members. Their behavior wasn't new or unusual, it occurred each year. And yet, there were those who somehow expected these particular family members to be different by the next family gathering. Needless to say, those expecting a difference were consistently frustrated by the end of the family event. At some point of observing this vicious cycle I decided to take a different posture; accepting that these family members are who they are without demand of change. Why? I realized my demand of others to change placed me in a powerless position and increased the likelihood of my frustration, because we have no power or ability to change another person. If the person does not agree to the change we require, he or she will not change.

So eventually I learned to assume the following posture: if her behavior wasn't harmful, I simply accepted it as is without demand of her being different – understanding that our dislike of someone's behavior doesn't make it wrong. I realized that it often felt wrong because I didn't like the behavior, or perhaps didn't understand it. But I also came to understand, just because it felt wrong, didn't automatically make it wrong.

On the other hand, if the behavior was potentially harmful, I went into a protective mode, shielding or defending those who could not protect themselves, along with protecting me. In many cases, I also went into a teaching mode, helping those who would listen and understand the impact of their actions. The most important lesson is "when people show me who they are, I believe them and act accordingly." What does this look like from a practical perspective? I either depend on or don't depend on, trust or don't trust, respect or don't respect, yield or don't yield. Again, I act accordingly based upon what the individual has shown herself to be over time. In essence, I accept the person for who she is currently, since I have no power to make her be otherwise. This statement is not to say that individuals lack the capacity to change. However, until I see, experience the change I believe the person to be who she has historically shown herself to be.

NOTE: I am also not saying we fail to hold each other accountable. We must be accountable to one another – the closer the relationship, the more accountability. However, accountability is not synonymous with judgment and demand of others being as we deem appropriate or simply want them to be. Accountability speaks more of a willingness to allow others to speak into our lives - sharing the good, bad and the ugly. Please know, however, those who have earned the right to hold us accountable have done so because they have previously shown that they have our best interest at heart. When individuals have loved and cared for us well they have earned the right to speak into our lives – to hold us accountable. I personally believe, if there is no love, there is no privilege. It is a privilege to hold others accountable, let's not take it for granted or abuse the right.

OPPORTUNITY FOR REFLECTIONS

CHAPTER SIX

SELF-APPRECIATION
& CELEBRATION

Appreciation is the key to love and care for ourselves. The more we practice self nurturing, the deeper the capacity to love and care for others.

-Kristin Louise Granger

The more you praise and celebrate your life, the more there is to celebrate.

- Oprah Winfrey

Appreciation is gratefulness for those parts of you that are to be celebrated, and a sobering awareness of the parts that warrant attention, followed by energy toward the necessary change. Even with the need to change some parts, it is time to celebrate the unique gift you are to this earth. Yes, you are a gift! Koty Bateman in *Promptings* states:

Every person reading this book has uniqueness in them. There are things in the world only you can do. There are people only you can reach. There is genius within you that only you have. I do think a lot of myself, and it's time you start doing the same. We are all destined for greatness, and anything less than that is an excuse. I choose not to live with excuses; I live with possibilities ... You have the ability to change the world with who you are.

Along the lines of Koty's statement, I believe that each of us is uniquely positioned to effectively speak to some small portion of the world. There are people in the world who need to hear your voice, to experience your positive presence in their lives. Because no other person is as uniquely designed to effectively speak into a particular person's life as you are, it is important to embrace the fact this is a portion of your life's purpose. Your uniqueness is to be appreciated and celebrated, not masked or apologized for. So ask yourself: "How am I different?" In what ways do you stand out within the crowd? This is not an attempt to say that anyone is better than another. I am only encouraging you to find and appreciate your unique parts.

As a university professor I sometimes shock my classes with this self-description during my introduction, "I am all that and a bag of chips" You can imagine the reactions to this statement coming from the person who will assign a final grade. However, those stares of horror and awkward smiles change when "I am all that and a bag of chips," is quickly followed with "And, I think the same about you." Boy you can feel the tension release in the room. I go on to complete the statement with, "I believe we are all precious gifts who have much to add to the betterment of society." Needless to say, this type of conversation changes the classroom atmosphere for the better. My primary message here is, you are uniquely gifted. Society needs you to embrace this notion so we can benefit from the gift of you.

Even after having engaged the previous chapters, for some, the idea of being a gift, precious or unique may be difficult to agree with. Perhaps it's difficult because of life choices, or possibly others' opinions of us causes appreciation to be challenging, or even worse, how we view ourselves leads to hesitation of personal appreciation and celebration. Please hear me: there is no time like the present to start celebrating and appreciating you. Let's debunk the lie that attempts to abort this final step in the process. Few people have lived in such a way that there is nothing worthy of appreciation and celebration. Too often the situation is that one has believed the lies spoken about their personal worth. If this is you, let's go to the place of untruths, the world of lies and deal with them. The truth of the matter is you are valuable simply because you are a living, breathing human being; that fact alone establishes worth. Your life matters and it is very likely that you already make a difference in others' lives.

Again, appreciation is gratefulness for those parts that are to be celebrated and a sobering awareness for that which warrants attention and energy toward change. Habbakuk 2:2 says to write the vision and make it plain. Koty Bateman learned from many of the positive thinking gurus about the power of vision. I don't believe in reinventing the wheel - when a technique has proven to be effective, why recreate another one. So let's do like so many before us and reinforce that which we desire by making lists (writing the vision). Here is an example...

Celebrating my Beneficial Ways of Being

I celebrate how I love others

I celebrate my awareness of being loved by God

I celebrate my gift of teaching

I celebrate the ways in which I care for me

I celebrate my ability to be faithful and
trustworthy in relationships

I celebrate my current level of self-love

I celebrate my abilities to adapt, learn, speak life and smile often

Celebrating Awareness of my Unbeneficial Ways of Being

(*It's important to write these statements in a way that
speaks to how you want to be. This acknowledges where you
are, but doesn't leave you in this state. This method points
you to the possible or desired future state of being.*)

I celebrate awareness of a need to improve in task completion

I celebrate awareness of a need to be determined
to speak kindly when I feel threatened

I celebrate awareness of my need to stop procrastinating

I celebrate awareness of my desire to lose
weight, become more physically fit

I celebrate awareness of a need to be less
stubborn and more flexible at times

You may be wondering about the "Awareness of Unbeneficial Ways of Being" list. Increased levels of self-love compel one to better your best. Since there is no perfect human being, the need for adapting and changing is ever present. The self-love journey is a lifelong process requiring awareness as a key to changing unbeneficial behavior.

To that end, take a moment to list all the things you don't like about yourself. Now, make a list of all that you like about yourself. In most cases, the "don't like" list was easier to construct and is longer than the "like" list. For some reason, there is this phenomenon where people are more comfortable and familiar with their weaknesses than strengths. However, the self-love perspective warrants a sobering look and comfort with both. It is the place of awareness that is the catalyst for empowerment to make choices about the varying aspects of us.

Note: It may also be necessary to lament over our unbeneficial ways of being (*please refer back to the earlier statement about the importance of not undertaking such an effort by yourself). Acknowledging failures, offenses, unproductive behavior, shortcomings, etc. is often very difficult and may lead to uncomfortable feelings. This is normal and healthy. It means that we are still humans who care about how we impact others and ourselves. However, we do not stay here. Remaining here too long can lead to other self-defeating behavior or states such as depression and giving up. We visit, long enough to gain insight, helping us to avoid making the same mistakes in the future, then we move on. A productive life is lived on purpose - possessing keen self-awareness, along with having an accurate awareness of others.

Remember we are still in the "Appreciation & Celebration" section of the book. Now, I would like you to celebrate the distinct individual you are. So answer this question discussed by John Maxwell in *Everyone Communicates, But Few Connect*: "How do you add value" by being uniquely you?

Let's make a list, Yes, another list – you are worth it!

Here is an example from my life.

> I add value
> through my ability to create emotionally safe environments
> by smiling often
> through my ability to multi-task, allowing me to help in many
> situations
> by admitting to my mistakes and being ok with my limitations
> by my determination to honor God and others in relationships
> by being trustworthy, loyal, a person of integrity and loving
> by freely giving of my resources

by speaking the truth in love, when necessary, and if kind

by being my best possible self and yet being ok when I fall short

by allowing others to help me, thereby showing that I need others

by loving well

Don't settle for a short list. Your ability to develop these celebratory lists and self-love are expected to grow together. As you become more accustomed to identifying all of your parts--not just the bad, but the good as well--it will become more natural to celebrate you.

About Me ... How I Add Value

My personal philosophy can be summed in an acronym PAP. It stands for People are Precious! I believe that every human being on this earth is precious. The caveat is some precious people must be medicated or incarcerated to protect all; however, in no way does this reality diminish our preciousness. From my perspective nothing changes the reality that each human is precious; not gender, age, socio economic status, ethnicity, religious preference, physical, mental status or educational attainment, or what one has done or failed to do. None of these affect one's state of preciousness. We are all precious!

This mental and heart posture, which I attempt to continually maintain, helps me treat others as I wish to be treated. It is not that I always accomplish this feat, but it is an ongoing goal. Viewing others as precious is a fairly easy state to achieve when they treat me well. The true test of character, however, comes when I am mistreated. Life has offered me many opportunities to test my personal philosophy: Do I really mean what I say? When others are lying on me, do I really believe they are precious? If I am cheated out of an opportunity, will I still see the culprit as precious? Do I see individuals as precious when they seem to have been created to be my personal irritation? Though there are times when I fail to accomplish this task, it yet remains to be my ongoing goal.

Pursuing this goal (seeing others as precious) positions me more often than not, to be added value in a majority of the situations I encounter.

Viewing others through a lens of preciousness bridles my tongue when I want to speak death and releases me to speak life instead. Have you ever noticed how it seems easier for people to make negative rather than positive comments? Our society appears to thrive from inflicting verbal harm on each other. However, I choose to look for the positive and speak it out loud. This often leads to awkwardness for the person receiving the word of affirmation, but I say it anyway. For instance, if I get into an elevator and notice someone with a beautiful smile, I tell him or her as much. When I have to say something that is potentially hurtful, I am very cautious and take time to carefully consider word choices, timing and motive before speaking.

About Me ... How I Celebrate Me

When I turned fifty, over three years ago now, I was tremendously grateful and excited to be a quarter of a century old. To me this was a milestone worth celebrating. So, for months I seized opportunities to declare, to whoever would listen, that I turned 50. I adopted a theme song *Freedom by Eddie James* and listened to it often. **The words warrant inclusion:**

FREEDOM

I wanna clap a little louder than before
I wanna sing a little louder than before
I wanna jump higher than before
I wanna shout louder than before
I wanna lift my hands higher than before
I wanna love you more than before
I wanna worship deeper than before
I gotta scream louder than before

I seized as many opportunities as possible to play this song for myself and all others who would listen.

My oldest sister was determined to give me a birthday party and many of my loved ones (family and friends) came to celebrate with me. That evening we uncorked many bottles of sparkling cider. Then, for the next couple of months I took a bottle of sparkling cider and plastic champagne flutes with me to varying places. One of my most enjoyable and memorable moments was walking into a classroom (as the professor) with bottles of sparkling and plastic flutes in hand. Now three things you must know to get a full sense of the moment are: (1) the students could not see the label on the bottle. At first glance it appeared as the professor walked into class with several bottles of wine, (2) they had no idea it was my birthday, so they weren't forearmed about potential celebrations, and (3) they were theology students as this particular place of employment was at a seminary. You can imagine the looks of bewilderment or shock upon my entrance. It was a wonderful time with great teaching moments.

During my celebration period, I came across many (particularly women) who were taken aback by my willingness to openly share my age. This is somewhat bewildering to me. Why? First of all the alternative to turning another year older is death, which I am not inviting before its time. Next, I do not have anything to gain by lying about my age. I want to engage people who accept me for who I am, at whatever age I may be. Finally, I don't want to be younger than I am, nor do I want to be older than I am. I have determined to be appreciative of each life stage and to make the most of the journey it brings.

Now, I'm not ignorant to the fact that a generation of women was taught to not tell your age. But I believe the teaching was out of ignorance. I in no way intend to offend anyone. So, why do I say this? Very simply, emotionally and psychologically healthy mothers don't typically teach their daughters to lie. For varying reasons, however, this was a common practice. I believe we know better today and when we know better, we can and hopefully do, do better.

So my encouragement: Let's be okay with all of who we are, including all the numbers that represent us; whether the numbers are representations of our age, dress or shoe size, number of children birthed or not, successes or failures. We are not the numbers. They do not speak to our worth. The numbers are simply representations of some aspect of us, but they are not us! Think about it this way. I wear a size 24 dress, but that is not who I am. That number represents my dress size, not my character, ability to love, think or act and certainly is not a reflection of my worth.

Being honest about all of me provides the liberty to fortify that, which is beneficial and work on changing all that is not. For instance, being a 53 year old African American woman who wears a 24 size dress could be problematic, given that diseases like hypertension, diabetes, and heart disease are common amongst us. So, I never settle with being a size 24 – often beginning a new plan to reduce the size. In addition, I never speak negatively to myself about being a size 24. I speak the truth and act accordingly. In whichever state I am, there are some things about me worth celebrating.

NOTHING TO APPRECIATE OR CELEBRATE

On the other hand, if you believe you have lived life in such a way that there is currently nothing to appreciate and/or celebrate, again, there is no time like the present to change things for the better. I strongly urge you to consider that reading this book has not been a coincidence. You have run into destiny and now have an opportunity and a tool to help you embark on a path of becoming a better you. Moving forward may require returning to the self-acceptance and forgiveness chapters: They offer instructions about acknowledging how we've engaged in self or other destructive behavior, as well as provide forward moving steps to release yourself and others for bondage that often accompanies life destructive behavior.

Please remember, arriving at self-love is not a destination but a life-long journey. The journey of self-love is a cyclical process whereby each pass takes one to deeper and deeper levels of self-love. As such, the book is written with an understanding of the possible need to revisit parts of the book at different times in life. Depending on life's situations and our responses to them, we may need to appreciate ourselves more during one season, and explore more of ourselves in another season. Either way, with each additional visit and practice, we are gaining deeper levels of self-love. So if appreciation and celebration is a struggle for you, go on, begin again. You are worth the time, effort and commitment necessary to arrive at an increased level of self-love.

OPPORTUNITY FOR REFLECTIONS

CHAPTER SEVEN

SELF-LOVE REVISITED
DON'T GET IT TWISTED: IT'S ABOUT YOU, BUT IT'S NOT *ONLY* ABOUT YOU!

Alone, all alone. Nobody, but nobody can make it out here alone.

- Maya Angelou

No man is an island: in and of itself.

- John Donne

At this point of the book, it is important to thoroughly discuss this notion of self-love and the necessary balance. John Donne, the English Clergyman and Poet coined the phrase, "No man is an island: in and of itself." Whereas on the one hand, this notion of self-love is a personal journey you alone can embark upon and endure. On the other hand, it unquestionably – at critical junctures in the process – involves others.

IT'S ALL ABOUT YOU

You alone can make the decision to acquire or improve upon the love you have for yourself. Self-love is one of the greatest gifts one can give. And, again, only you can give this precious gift. To that end, it is all about you. It is about your willingness to embark on a personal explorative journey leading you to recall things that have long been forgotten, and to unearth that which you potentially have no conscious awareness of – yet once surfaced rings with familiarity. It's about you moving from discovery to forgiveness, letting yourself and others off the hook. It is about accepting all that was unearthed in the discovery process, and all that was forgiven. It is about learning to appreciate the you of today, while in anticipation and celebration of how you are to become.

Whereas the self-love journey is uniquely your own, you do not travel it alone. Others may not direct the process, but because "No man is an island …" they certainly influence the process and are impacted by your journey.

It's Not All About You

Along with embracing all of you, it is imperative to avoid allowing this journey to lead one to function from a narcissistic, self-centered way of being. Yes, all previous chapters were written with the intent of leading you towards increased levels of self-love. In no way however, is this pursuit to be at the expense of loving others, quite the contrary. Actually, self-love increases one's ability to love others. There is a positive correlation between loving self and loving others. As we love ourselves more, our capacity to love others increases.

Until now our conversation has focused inwardly, to experience an introspective journey. "Don't get it twisted" is a way of saying don't confuse the pursuit of self-love with permission to devalue others. Like self-love is a gift, so is community. Being a part of a safe, rewarding community promotes relationally healthy living.

Community powerfully contributes to who we are and become. We are born with particular traits and bents toward life, those traits and bents interact with our environment and we become. Community has the ability to symbolically wrap us in the warmest of blankets (insulate), or snare us in the prickliest life fabrics (imprison). Regardless of how community has impacted us, at some point, we decide how we will engage and be engaged by community. What is your impact on community?

Remember that self-love compels us to be better for ourselves and for others. So here's the question: are you "added value" to your community? Do you add to its growth, healthy development and vitality? Are your deposits such that others are better when they have engaged you? Or do you leave trails of despair, and disappointment?

Like self-love, healthy community is a precious gift to have, one worth protecting and preserving, one worth emulating if it exists, or fostering if it does not. Perhaps you are asking, what is healthy community?

Let's look at elements that make for a healthy community:

❖ Safe – individuals are free to be themselves without constant fear of rejection, retaliation, judgment or betrayal. It is an environment that celebrates unique ways of being and accepts as is without demand to conform. Individuals who engage within these types of environments are safe from physical, psychological, emotional, and spiritual abuse; one is safe enough to show the true self - strengths, weaknesses, desires, hopes and dreams. Safe does not mean without harm of any kind. As humans we fall short and harm one another all the time. However, the harm occurring within safe environments is without intent or malice; they are simply acts of ignorance, bad judgments or poor choices that happen to lead to harm. When harm is inflicted, those who engage within a safe environment swiftly move towards amends –quickly they work to right the wrong.

❖ Acceptance – the environment understands we are uniquely different and accepts individuals for who they are. This is not to say there isn't a desire of change. For instance, a mother greatly desires her teenager to keep a clean room; a husband wishes his wife wouldn't spend so much on credit cards and a friend is often irritated by her friend's lack of punctuality. These examples share in common a desire for one party to be different in some way. However, the desire for change doesn't equate rejection or mistreatment of the person; it speaks of preference. The mother, husband and friend desire their loved one to be different, but they don't mistreat them because they are not.

❖ Reciprocity – healthy relationships include both processes of giving and receiving. Misuse and abuse occurs when there is a constant imbalance of giving and receiving. Life or relational stages and situations dictate the balance of giving and receiving. For instance, parents spend a good portion of their time giving to younger children – this is to be expected in a healthy parent/child relationship. However, as children proceed through developmental stages, their need for parental involvement decreases and the balance of give and receive begins to level out – when things are in good working order. An absence of this balance often leads to unproductive situations of perhaps misuse, abuse or an unhealthy dependence. When the imbalance is perpetuated by an over-indulging parent, codependent, enmeshed relationships are created; when perpetuated by the child (they refuse to give back), a misuse or abusive environment is fostered.

The diagram below depicts the realities of relational reciprocity. If selfishness is at one extreme of the continuum and selflessness at the other, what belongs in the center? The center is represented by self-care.

Image 1 depicts a balance of each statebut an unrealistic reality. Rarely are we perfectly balanced between these two states.

Image 2 depicts an imbalance towards selflessness, which is often necessary during parenting years, caring for aging parents, support of family and friends during crises situations, etc.

Image 3 depicts an imbalance toward selfishness, generally occurring when one is in need; representing situations of personal loss (death, divorce, loss of job), physical ailments, emotional challenges, physical or mental exhaustion, etc.

When things are balanced (self-care), there is a healthy dose of give (selflessness) and take (selfishness). Rarely does life remain in this balanced state, though. Consequently, a healthy depiction is truly reflected in our understanding of the need to adjust based upon the current life situation. We are to strive to keep a healthy balance of selfishness and selflessness. We are not practicing self-care if we neglect others when they are in need; conversely, we are not practicing self-care if we neglect ourselves when we are in need.

- ❖ Accountability – represents mutual submission and respect where community members are answerable to one another.
- ❖ Commitment & Responsibility– both are reflected through decision-making and choice. Individuals choose to be obligated to one another's well-being and act in ways to promote betterment.
- ❖ Love – a desiring and doing of that which is best for one another. Best may equate to grace, hugs and kisses, discipline, confrontation (I prefer the use of care-fronting), limitation, releasing, and holding on tighter, etc.

There is no perfect community! Yet, there are healthy communities that in many ways resemble the previously described. In no way is this presentation intended to be an exhaustive list. I'm sure you can come up with your own list of elements that are representative of a healthy community. Whereas, there are healthy communities, the fact remains there are too many toxic communities that leave life-long scars. So whether this list or another, the need for an increase of healthy communities warrant attention discovering what one looks like. Is your community healthy? What are the primary elements operating in your community?

I am not blind to the fact that many have not been born into, reared in, or are currently a part of a healthy community. All is not lost. Please know it can begin with you! When we recognize the absence of health, it is time to change the environment. Hear this, you are currently a part of a system. Systems theory states, any change to the system impacts the system (Corey, 2013). There is no guarantee of how the system will change; just that it cannot remain the same once any part has changed.

ABOUT ME … HOW I EFFECTED CHANGE IN MY FAMILY SYSTEM

If you had an opportunity to engage my family today, you would witness ongoing hugs, kisses, varying types of embraces and touches, kind words (sometimes not so kind words intended to be kind – we are working on that), "I love you" is stated often, compliments and lots and lots of laughter.

Now if we were to rewind prior to the early 1980s, the scene would be quite different. Growing up, although we loved each other, it was rarely stated and we weren't at all very "touchy feely." Rarely were there hugs upon greeting or departure and there was little affectionate touching or random words of kindness.

In 1981 I left Detroit and went away to Tennessee for college. This was the first time in my life being far away from my family, as well as my first visit to Tennessee. My family wasn't financially positioned to accompany me to this strange place, nor were they able to visit. Needless to say, I missed my family. I so longed to see them that upon my return I had this great need to embrace, and look upon them – to simply be in their company. Since these weren't normal acts amongst the adults (and thus would have felt rather awkward if initiated), I showered my affections on my young nieces and nephews. This is how they tell the story:

"We were playing at the corner on the lawn of the church and see auntie coming down the street. Immediately we say oh no run, auntie's coming, and she is going to want to hug and kiss us."

This is hilarious! I get so tickled when I think of my nieces and nephews running to hide so they could avoid my unfamiliar and therefore (at that time) uncomfortable displays of affection.

Certainly, they didn't share this with me at the time, and I so missed them that I would never have noticed their awkwardness about my new way of being. Well this continued for my two-year stay at Tennessee State University and by the time I made my way home to stay, the behavior had begun to take root and spread beyond the children. I call this the *Woods Kissing and Hugging Contagion*.

To see us today, none would think there was a time when this behavior was foreign to our family. Today, entering a room and neglecting to embrace generally denotes some type of problem – someone is at odds with someone else. This way of kinds words, embracing and safe tender touches is NOW our normal way of being and doing and I truly believe we as a family are better off because of it.

What am I saying ...

As humans we are in constant need of safe touch – some require more or less than others, but studies support the need nonetheless. If this is not a common or even acceptable practice within your community, you become the change agent by modeling the preferred behavior. I did this for my community and you have the ability to do the same for yours. Start with the easy targets and go from there. Believe me when I say, it is worth it. The primary reason we are uncomfortable with safe touch is because we have not experienced it and, therefore, we aren't used to it-- or because we have experienced unsafe touch. Either way, don't let this discomfort or the past negative experiences keep you from obtaining one of life's treasures – connecting on a physical level with those we care for or love.

Perhaps you've read all or parts of this book and yet do not believe that obtaining or increasing self-love is possible for you. To that I say, as Henry Ford, "*Whether you think you can, or you think you can't--you're right.*" Ultimately, living a life of self-love is a choice. No one can choose this way of life for you or me. In this, we are the captains of our own ships, the masters of our own souls. What choice will you make for your soul?

A final word of encouragement...

Give yourself permission to be ok with the person you are today, so you can get about the business of becoming the better you of tomorrow; and don't forget to LOVE yourself and others well! Few things in life will benefit you better.

I sincerely believe, we have been given the gift of life. Life is precious, and at the very least warrants the the gift of increase self-love. What say you? Will you do what is necessary to increase self-love? The choice is yours and yours alone.

Love well my friend.

FINAL OPPORTUNITY FOR REFLECTIONS

REFERENCES

Balswick, J. O. & Balswick, J. K. (1999). *The family: A Christian perspective on the contemporary home.* Grand Rapids, MI: Baker Publishing Group.

Bateman, K. (2011) *Promptings: Your inner guide to making a difference.* Salt Lake City, UT: Eagle One Publishing.

Bracy, B. (2013). Preached Message: Shiloh Deliverance Church International: Detroit, MI.

Comer, R. J. (2013). *Fundamental of abnormal psychology.* New York, NY: Worth Publishers.

Corey, G. (2013). *Theory and practice of counseling and psychotherapy.* Belmont, CA: Brooks/Cole

Hill, N. (1997). Keys to success: The 17 principles of personal achievement. New York: Penguin Books.

The Holy Bible

Hockenbury, D., H. & Hockenbury, S, E. (2012). *Psychology.* Belmont, CA: Worth Publishers.

James, Eddie. (2011). *Freedom.* Loganville, GA: Fresh Wine Records.

Kiyosaki, Robert. (2015). *Rich dad, poor dad.* Plata Publishing

Pietzker, Mary, A. (1872). *Miscellaneous poems.* Griffith and Farran of London.

GLOSSARY OF TERMS

Accountability. Represents mutual submission and respect where community members are answerable to one another.

Acceptance. The environment understands we are uniquely different and accepts individuals for who they are.

Be. Represents being psychologically, emotionally, and relationally authentic.

Behavioral or expressive response. Represents what you do. For instance we generally smile when happy, frown and/or cry when sad and flee when afraid. These responses are always visible to others.

Commitment & Responsibility. Both are reflected through decision-making and choice. Individuals choose to be obligated to one another's well-being and act in ways to promote betterment.

Feelings/Emotions. An inner spontaneous reaction to a person, place, thing or situation or the soul's response to life.

Forgiveness. Synonyms for forgiveness are to pardon, give clemency, to exonerate, give amnesty or mercy.

Love. A desiring and doing of that which is best for one another. Best may equate to grace, hugs and kisses, discipline, confrontation (I prefer the use of care-fronting), limitation, releasing, and holding on tighter, etc.

Physiological response. Represents your body's response. It may be stomach queasiness, rapid eye movement, racing heart, goose bumps, etc. These responses are often not visible to others.

Reciprocity. Healthy relationships include both processes of giving and receiving.

Safe. Individuals are free to be themselves without constant fear of rejection, retaliation, judgment or betrayal.

Self-exploration. (1) Tell yourself *the whole truth,* (2) Be intentional about identifying your ever changing emotions, (3) Pay attention to your physical responses to internal and external experiences and (4) Engage in activities that will increase your relational awareness.

Self-love. An accepting, valuing and embracing of one's entire self, inclusive of an activating awareness, which motivates toward the need to continually change for the better.

Subjective experience. Represents your unique way of experiencing a situation. Although we can have the same external experience, we very often have a different internal experience. It is perception. We simply see things differently. This is because we have different backgrounds.

QUOTES, POEM, SCRIPTURES & SONG

Man cannot love that which he does not know.

           - James Allen

Only by much searching and mining are gold and diamonds obtained, and man can find every truth connected with his being if he will dig deep into the mine of his soul.

           - James Allen

Alone, all alone. Nobody, but nobody can make it out here alone.

           - Maya Angelou

What we say subconsciously becomes our reality.

           - Kody Bateman

Every person reading this book has uniqueness in them. There are things in the world only you can do. There are people only you can reach. There is genius within you that only you have. I do think a lot of myself, and it's time you start doing the same. We are all destined for greatness, and anything less than that is an excuse. I choose not to live with excuses; I live with possibilities ... You have the ability to change the world with who you are.

- Kody Bateman

Self-acceptance is my refusal to be in an adversarial relationship with myself.

- Nathaniel Brand

No man is an island: in and of itself.

- John Donne

Whether you think you can or think you can't, you're right.

- Henry Ford

Being honest with your self is good exercise.

- Sigmund Freud

Appreciation is the key to love and care for ourselves. The more we practice self nurturing, the deeper the capacity to love and care for others.

-Kristin Louise Granger

Whatever you think today becomes what you are tomorrow.

- Napoleon Hill

An emotion is a complex psychological state that involves three distinct components: a subjective experience, a physiological response, and a behavioral or expressive response.

- Hockenbury & Hockenbury

For all have sinned, and come short of the glory of God; (Romans 3:23).

> - Holy Bible.

Leave there thy gift before the altar, and go thy way; first be reconciled to thy brother, and then come and offer thy gift. (Mathew 5:2).

> - Holy Bible.

If it be possible, as much as lieth in you, live peaceably with all men. (Romans 12:18).

> - Holy Bible.

For as he thinketh in his heart, so is he: Eat and drink, saith he to thee; but his heart is not with thee. (Proverb 23:7).

> - Holy Bible.

And the LORD answered me, and said, Write the vision, and make it plain upon tables, that he may run that readeth it. (Habbakuk 2:2).

> - Holy Bible.

Freedom. [Song]

> - Eddie James.

It's not what you say out of your mouth that determines your life, it's what you whisper to yourself that has the most power!

> - Robert Kiosaki

If we really want to love, we must learn how to forgive.

- Mother Theresa

God grant me the serenity to accept the things I cannot change, the courage to change the things I can, and the wisdom to know the difference.

- Reinhold Niebuhr

The greatest trap in our life is not success, popularity or power, but self-rejection.

- Henri Nouwen

Is it True, Is it Necessary, Is it Kind. [Poem]

- Mary Ann Pietzker

The mind, just like the body is susceptible to illness.

- Johann Weyer

The more you praise and celebrate your life, the more there is to celebrate.

- Oprah Winfrey

You will begin to heal when you let go of past hurts, forgive those who have wronged you and learn to forgive yourself for your mistakes.

- Author Unknown

INDEX of NOTED WORDS and PHRASES

W

Y

CPSIA information can be obtained
at www.ICGtesting.com
Printed in the USA
FFOW05n2109181016

9 781524 640804